JOURNEY TO EARTHLAND

The Great Transition to
Planetary Civilization

PAUL RASKIN

Tellus Institute
11 Arlington Street
Boston, Massachusetts 02116
www.tellus.org

ISBN: 978-0-9978376-0-5

For the vision-keepers—yesterday's trailblazers to a world made whole, today's multitudes carrying it forward, and tomorrow's travelers who may glimpse the destination.

CONTENTS

◇◇◇◇◇◇◇

AUTHOR'S PREFACE

To paraphrase Ray Bradbury, I write not to describe the future, but to prevent it. Peering into our respective crystal balls, you and I may see different worlds ahead, but surely we can agree on this: we have much to prevent. Any candid appraisal of global prospects in this century confronts, among other portents, climate change, cultural polarization, economic volatility, resource depletion, and social disparity. Whether these threats leave us feeling merely uneasy or trapped on a detonating powder keg, the question of the future demands answers.

Some of the most important stories of any age remain unwritten: the averted futures that might have been. In my lifetime, the world has dodged megaton bullets and colossal bullies. In many ways these were tragic years of genocidal cruelty, Cold War flirtations with annihilation, and double-time march to the edge of ecocide. Even so, it could have been much worse had fascism triumphed or a nuclear war erupted or an environmental movement not slowed the rivers of poison. Civilization survived to stagger forward—to what?

Wanting to play a part in the answer, I left the academy in the 1970s and, with a small group of like-minded colleagues, started an institute committed to rigorous research in service to progressive social change. The Tellus Institute conducted thousands of projects throughout the world on a full spectrum of environmental, resource, and social issues. My own work evolved in congruence with the rapidly changing agenda of a world in transition: energy, water, climate change, ecosystems, sustainability, globalization, scenarios of the future.

In the course of grappling with problems of ever-growing complexity and interconnection, my perspective broadened and deepened. I came to see the astonishing developments of the past several decades as chapters in an overarching narrative—discrete signals of a unitary transformation in the way the world operates and the planet functions. Looking through narrow apertures, observers focused on single dimensions of this holistic shift—economic globalization, climate change, the information revolution, transnational terrorism, cosmopolitan culture, and so on. The world, awash in specialized reports, was starved of systemic examinations and panoptic foresight.

In 1990, prompted by the deficit of big-picture conceptual frameworks, I organized the PoleStar Project to imagine and model contrasting long-range futures for the global social-ecological system. This work led to the creation of the international, interdisciplinary Global Scenario Group (GSG), which I co-organized in 1995, and the launch of a multi-year research program that strengthened my conviction that a world-historical transformation was underway. The essence of this Planetary Phase of Civilization (our term for the emerging era) is the deepening interdependence binding humanity and Earth into a single community of fate. As it unfolds in this century, the drama of social-ecological evolution will play out on a world stage as an enveloping sphere of crisis and struggle.

The GSG's valedictory 2002 essay, *Great Transition: The Promise and Lure of the Times Ahead*, summarized these ideas and urged a fundamental shift in the paradigm of development—indeed, in the very meaning of human progress. A Great Transition would make solidarity, fulfillment, and resilience the heart and soul of human endeavor. In the tumultuous years since its publication, scientific understanding has burgeoned, consciousness has evolved, and astonishing and terrible phenomena have occurred. Who knew we would have powerful computers in our pockets and Big Data in our living rooms, terrorized cities and awful wars, financial bubbles and great recessions, Arab Springs and then bitter falls, and climate impacts toward the extreme end of the uncertainty range?

Still, the principal takeaways of *Great Transition* endure: the concept of the Planetary Phase, the mounting peril along the conventional path, the real, growing risk of barbarization, and the possibility nonetheless of a turn toward a future of enriched lives and a healthy planet. Because we now know more than we did in 2002, including the ever-intensifying, urgent need for systemic change, the time for this sequel has arrived.

Journey to Earthland revisits and updates the conceptual framework of *Great Transition*, and goes on to elaborate three core areas, drawing from my publications and presentations over the past decade. First, the essay clarifies the meaning of the historic juncture, introducing the idea of "Earthland" to characterize the nascent supranational community now stirring. Second, it focuses on the critical question of collective action, whereby a vast and plural "global citizens movement" becomes the key social actor for carrying the transformation forward.

Third, it offers a vision of a resilient civilization, a world *in potentia* on the far side of a Great Transition—if together we can take the helm and navigate wisely through an unsettled century.

I have had the good fortune that my work has required reflection on the larger significance of this fateful century. Out of these reflections came *Journey*, at once essay, narrative, and manifesto, comingling genres in seeking to persuade the critical intellect, stimulate the social imagination, and inspire collective action. I offer these meditations at a critical juncture: the odyssey of planetary transition is underway, yet the ultimate destination still depends on human decisions and struggles to come. Acting to prevent the futures we dread is where our work must begin. But survival is not sufficient: the larger task is to foster the finer Earthland we and our descendants deserve.

◇◇◇◇◇◇◇

PROLOGUE
BOUND TOGETHER

We are bound together on a precarious passage to a land unknown and unnamed. Even a stray dog, as Hannah Arendt once noted, has better odds of surviving when given a name. Likewise, the global future—the place to which we are headed—needs an identity to encourage us to own and care for it. A suitable coinage ought to conjure the nature of the beast: a borderless community intertwining the destinies of all earthly creatures, living and unborn. Like a superordinate country, this incipient formation is encircling all existing countries in an integral sphere of land, sea, and sky. Let us call this proto-country Earthland.

Without flight plan or clear destination, we are winging through a blizzard of uncertainty to this different world. The shape of the new order off the bow is not yet visible, while the old one, along with its familiar disappointments and consolations, fades astern. Longing for the *terra firma* of the past persists, but there is no turning back or deplaning on a craft equipped with forward gears only and warning lights at each door that flash No Exit.

On board, white-knuckled passengers are awakening to their existential quandary. They tremulously inquire about location and direction, but bewildered cabin attendants can provide only disjointed information and unpersuasive reassurances. In the cockpit, the insouciant captains cast desultory glances at the flight screens or doze, awaiting instructions from perplexed navigators.

These unnerving circumstances elicit the full arsenal of psychological responses: discounting dangers in sweet denial, finding distraction in passing amusements and baubles, and seeking succor in the false panaceas of free markets, religious rapture, or individual beatitude. Some despondent souls confront their plight open-eyed, but seeing no way out, turn away in fatalistic despair. Most are just trying to muddle through, keeping their heads down and hoping for the best.

These are natural, human responses to living in a disturbing and perplexing time. Yet denial, distraction, and despair—the three D's of an anxious culture—cannot proffer insight or solution. Racing into a dubious future, we do not have the luxury to just go along for the ride. Were we mere passengers on this expedition, then the denouement, whether barbaric or enlightened, would warrant only speculative interest. The trip would end, and we would disembark. But we are more: our ways of being and acting set the course and influence the outcome on this planet, our only home.

Along the way, indifference and quiescence are surely choices as much as awareness and action, all choices that will shape the destination. These high stakes demand urgent attention, and accordingly, more of us are growing alert and inquisitive. The passenger's passive query—Where are we going?—has no cogent answer. Instead, we pose the traveler's salient questions of vision and intention: Where do we want to go? How do we get there?

The search for meaning and hope in human destiny is fundamental to the human experience, the *sine qua non* of a species that remembers and imagines, dreams and dreads. Fables of providence have infused the mythology of all cultures, expressing a transcendent longing for guidance and redemption. While the modern mindset harnesses the prophetic imagination to the rigors of secular knowledge, the yearning persists for compelling narratives of who we are and what we might become.

To what previously may have animated speculation about the future—curiosity, advantage, anxiety, a search for meaning—can be added a thoroughly contemporary concern: passing an undiminished world to posterity. The disturbances to the biosphere that recent and current generations have set in motion, past critical thresholds, are difficult to reverse. Smoldering social antagonisms can become engraved indelibly in institutional and cultural memory. Crises manifest gradually or suddenly, then linger long. Faint pleas to temper them can be heard, if we listen, from all the voiceless ones: from grandchildren unborn to grandparents-to-be, from the excluded and impoverished to the entrenched and privileged, and from imperiled fellow creatures to the human species.

The dream of a congenial world commonwealth has long sparked the social imagination, yet throughout our fractured and bloody history it has remained a utopian abstraction. The aspirants have been unable to delineate a practical enterprise of social and cultural evolution to bring the castle-in-the-air down to earth—until now. In the interdependent twenty-first century, the cosmopolitan vision confronts us, not as an unreachable ideal, but as a historical imperative—and unprecedented opportunity.

Immersed in the turbulence of a world in transition, we have difficulty discerning the larger pattern that unifies and gives meaning to the extraordinary changes unfolding around us, much like creatures of the sea unable to perceive the vast and roiling ocean in which they swim. Fortunately, we are not fish (if unfortunately for them). We can exercise intellect and imagination to assess the predicament and set course. The journey to Earthland has begun, interrupting historical continuity, weakening old social structures, and loosening cultural strictures, thereby expanding the scope for human choice and freedom.

In this key moment, collective action can make a revolutionary difference in the quest for a convivial and resilient planetary civilization. Somewhere ahead, barely discernible beyond the mist and tumult, lies a land of seven oceans, seven continents, seven billion people, and seven wonders at every turn, a place where lives are rich and nature redolent. Drifting toward the abyss, we still can turn, with that world to gain.

◇◇◇◇◇◇◇

PART I
DEPARTURE: INTO THE MAELSTROM

The journey begins with the unsettling sense in the air of living in a dangerous and pivotal time. All the disruption and upheaval we confront are the birth pangs of the global entity herein christened Earthland. We can observe her embryonic form and speculate about her ultimate shape, but cannot foretell what sort of creature will be born, only that a long ordeal of growing pains lies ahead. Much depends on us, the guardians of her future, who are duty bound to find fresh answers to core questions: Who are we? How shall we live? Which Earthland?

The long prelude

Out of the cosmos

The main focus of this essay is on the meaning of the present and anatomy of the future, not the past. Still, to better gauge where we are and might go, we had best pause at the outset to recall where we have been. After all, Janus, the god of transition, simultaneously gazes backwards and forwards. So too must we be mindful that today is a moving threshold where yesterday meets tomorrow.

The broadest of perspectives can locate the shift underway on planet Earth as the most recent scene in a vast pageant of cosmic emergence. A cosmological panorama takes us beyond the ambit of daily life and beyond even the larger compass of human history, offering a vantage point for pondering the contemporary predicament. A reminder of where we are in the immensity of space, the eons of time, and the majestic evolution of existence, this wide vista cultivates a sense of awe and humility, stirring resolve to renew the vitality of our precious island of life. Such reflections bring into focus a transcendent challenge: to navigate toward a new order of complexity in our corner of the universe, a flourishing and resilient global society.[1]

The story of the cosmos begins nearly 14 billion years ago with the colossal energy eruption of the Big Bang. From the primal chaos of this prodigious event, structures consolidated in distinct stages, each adding new complexity to the grand unfolding of being: quarks and basic particles formed from the cauldron of radiant energy in the first fraction of a second; simple atoms stabilized after some 300,000 years as the universe cooled; galaxies coalesced around random asymmetries in matter distribution, eventually giving birth to stars and planets; and about 3.8 billion years ago, life appeared on Earth, opening a new chapter in the story of the universe.

Biological evolution has been a wondrous adventure of tenacity and inventiveness through titanic episodes of extinction and proliferation. In the fullness of evolutionary time, creatures with brains appeared, enjoying enhanced ability to repel danger and secure sustenance. Eventually, our diminutive mammalian forebears entered the stage, minor characters scurrying inconspicuously among larger and smarter Mesozoic contemporaries. Somehow, they found niches through the long reigns of the trilobites, fish, and reptiles. The actuarial probability of survival for these early mammals could not have been good, and the odds of hitting the jackpot in the lottery of evolution very long indeed.

Everything changed some 65 million years ago when Earth collided with an enormous asteroid, the single most cataclysmic day on this planet. This 10 kilometer *deus ex machina* from outer space struck with the force of a billion Hiroshima-size bombs, abruptly altering the scenery, plot, and cast of characters in the theater of natural history. The impact lifted immense dust clouds that blocked the sun and destroyed plant life. The death knell for the imperious dinosaurs (and three-quarters of then existing species) was the sound of opportunity for our furry ancestors, who made a fine living scavenging the insects and snails that flourished on the massive detritus of the global killing fields.

At the dawning of the Cenozoic Era, to be mammalian and small was highly adaptive. Multiplying and diversifying, they populated the Class Mammalia with innumerable design variations for warm-blooded and lung-breathing animals. The grandeur of that variety, from schooner-sized whales to pinkie-sized bumblebee bats, remains on display in the 5,000 or so extant mammalian species still clinging to the shrunken habitats of today's ecologically impoverished planet.

The second Big Bang

One uncommonly dexterous line—the primates—proved particularly consequential, giving rise to hominids, the first bipedal, tool-developing mammals. These brainy, social creatures jumped onto evolution's fast track and never looked back. The advent of human consciousness marked both a culmination and an inception: the capstone of biological evolution and the cornerstone of social evolution.

The appearance of human culture set off a second Big Bang in the generation of novel forms of existence in the known universe. Cultural evolution (including technology, social structures, rituals, and symbols) entered into a reciprocal dance with physical and cognitive evolution. Selection for tool-making, language, and social cooperation produced beings of unprecedented ingenuity and adaptability. At each moment, the cumulative heritage of ideas, institutions, inventions, and artifacts formed a springboard for accelerated social change, leaving in the dust the far more gradual processes of biological and geophysical evolution. The power of culture to mold and control the environment liberated humanity from dependence on narrow ecological niches, allowing congenitally preprogrammed behavior to give way to more malleable, historically constructed forms of conduct and association.

In three million years, a mere tick of the geological clock, the primitive sentience of early humans evolved into the higher consciousness of our anatomically modern ancestors some 200,000 years ago. A creature was born that carried the awesome power—and heavy burden—of introspection and reason. This was a luminous and fateful moment in the long saga of cosmic emanation; when it begot a primate able to contemplate the mystery of existence, the universe lit up to itself.

The arrival of modern humans, the last surviving hominid, brought the new phenomenon of human history to the unfolding scene, and with it a qualitatively different kind of transition: the movement between historical epochs. The most far-reaching of these social shifts were "great transitions" that altered the entire socio-cultural matrix, yielding new relationships among people and between society and nature. At these junctures, reinforcing processes of change rippled across multiple dimensions—technology, consciousness, and institutions—and weakened existing regulatory structures and social norms.

Of course, societies did not always survive these systemic ruptures; indeed, most civilizations of the past have fallen and vanished, spectacles of collapse that fascinate anew in our own time of vulnerability. But when they do not crumble, a fading order gestates a successor society, setting in motion a fresh dynamic of social evolution. Through mechanisms of conquest and assimilation, change radiates gradually from centers of novelty, although earlier eras can long survive in places that are physically remote and culturally isolated. Today's multitiered world overlays globalized dynamics across a mosaic of modern, pre-modern, and even remnants of Stone Age cultures.

Naturally, the course of history cannot be neatly organized as schoolbook timelines with sharp ticks demarcating well-defined epochs. Real history is an intricate and irregular process conditioned by specific local factors, chance, serendipity, and human volition. Various periodization criteria, such as the dominant political regime, major technology, and mode of production, offer complementary insights, but only partial truths. Moreover, perceptions of social change depend on the granularity of the historical lens through which we peer. Zooming in on finer spatial resolutions and shorter time frames provides greater detail; zooming out brings longer-term, larger-scale processes into focus.

Macro-shifts

A long view of the broad contours of the human experience reveals two sweeping macro-transformations. The first occurred roughly 10,000 years ago when Stone Age culture gave rise to Early Civilization. The second saw Early Civilization yield to the Modern Era over the last millennium.[2]

Now, the Modern Era itself confronts a deep structural crisis induced by its contradictions and limitations: perpetual growth on a finite planet, political fragmentation in an interdependent world, widening chasms between the privileged and the excluded, and a stifling culture of consumerism. In our time, an exhausted modernity is relinquishing the stage. A third macro-shift in the human condition is underway with implications as far-reaching as those of previous great transformations. History has entered the *Planetary Phase of Civilization.*

Scanning the contours of change across Stone Age, Early Civilization, Modern Era, and Planetary Phase epochs reveals a broad tendency for society to become more extensive and elaborate. Societal complexity (the number of variables needed to describe roles and relationships, and the degree of connectedness) increases over the course of these transitions. Each emergent phase absorbs and transforms its antecedents, adding novel attributes, greater intricacy, and new dynamics (see following figure). The characteristic unit of social organization moves from the highly local to the global, overlaying new forms on preexisting ones. The economic basis shifts from Stone Age hunting and gathering to the highly diversified and far-reaching globalized commerce of this century. Communications innovations— language, writing, printing, and information technology—usher in progressively more powerful modes of social intercourse.

The complexification and enlargement of society also quickens the pace of social evolution. Just as historical change moves more rapidly than biological change (and far more rapidly than geological change), so, too, is history itself accelerating. As the figure suggests, the Stone Age endured about 100,000 years; Early Civilization, roughly 10,000 years; and the Modern Era, now drawing to a close, began to stir nearly 1,000 years ago. If the Planetary Phase were to play out over 100 years, this sequence of exponentially decreasing timespans would persist. Whether this long pattern of acceleration is mere coincidence or manifestation of an underlying historical principle, the fact remains that the vortex of change now swirls around us with unprecedented urgency.

Phases of Human History

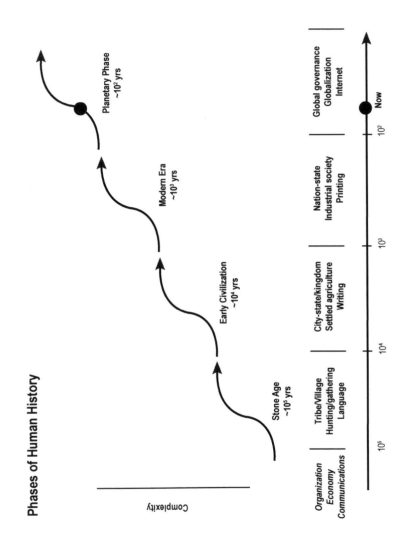

Complexity

Stone Age
~10^5 yrs

Early Civilization
~10^4 yrs

Modern Era
~10^3 yrs

Planetary Phase
~10^2 yrs

Organization
Economy
Communications

Tribe/Village
Hunting/gathering
Language

City-state/kingdom
Settled agriculture
Writing

Nation-state
Industrial society
Printing

Global governance
Globalization
Internet

10^5 10^4 10^3 10^2 **Now**

The Planetary Phase

A unitary formation

An extraterrestrial, observing developments on the third rock from the sun, would note with astonishment the quick rise to dominance of a single two-legged species. In a flicker of historical time, humanity has become a geological force, its once diminutive footprint grown to the scale of the planet. We are on the cusp of a new era, and its defining feature is that the globe itself is becoming the locus of social evolution and contending forms of consciousness.

Before our eyes, the world grows ever more complex in a blur of social and environmental change. Circuits of almost everything—goods, money, people, information, ideas, conflict, pathogens, effluvia—spiral round the planet farther and faster. Multiple interweaving threads of connectivity lengthen, strengthen, and thicken, forming the ligature of an integrated social-ecological system.

Whether denied, welcomed, or feared, a phenomenon of extreme significance is in progress, irrevocably transforming our lives and the planet. Heretofore, the world could be reasonably approximated as a set of semi-autonomous entities—states, ecosystems, cultures, territories—subject to external interactions. Now, as a superordinate system forms and global-scale processes increasingly influence the operation and stability of subsystems, such reductive partitioning becomes inaccurate and misleading.

The crystallizing global system comprises differentiated, interacting subsystems: economic, environmental, technological, cultural, and political. Transnational corporations have spun far-flung webs of production nodes and distribution channels, spewed rivers of international capital, and generated a bewildering array of financial instruments for speculative investment. The human transformation of nature has reached the level of the biosphere—the thin planetary shell that supports all life. The revolution in information and communication technology has compressed cultural and physical distance, penetrating remote societies and expanding cross-border networks and communities. Governments have created new international structures of dialogue (and occasionally governance), their number and diversity synchronized to proliferating challenges. The porosity of traditional geographic and cultural boundaries generates new fissures of conflict among powerful states and with non-state actors.

The Planetary Phase is entangling people and places in one global system with one shared destiny. Observers highlight different aspects—economics, corporations, climate change, health, technology, terrorism, civil society, governance, culture—all introduced by the modifier "global." Looking through specialized windows, economists see "globalization," technologists spotlight digital connectivity, environmentalists foreground the transformation of nature by human action, and geologists proclaim the arrival of the Anthropocene, a new geological age. Heterodox social scientists suggest other sobriquets: the Econocene dominated by the false ideology of neoclassical economics or the Capitalocene defined by capitalist relations of production and power.[3] Meanwhile, visionary philosophers and theologians point to signs of an emerging global ethos, while realpolitik types see only clashes of civilizations and great powers.

Each of these apertures on the human condition illuminates a critical aspect of the social-ecological whole, but rather than independent phenomena, these aspects are varied manifestations of a unitary transformation process. The Planetary Phase infuses the old adage of systems theory—the whole is more than the sum of its parts—with fresh meaning: there is something fundamentally new on the face of the earth. The global system and its components shape one another in a complex and reciprocal dance that changes both the whole and its parts.

Global climate change, driven by an infinitude of local actions, feeds back to alter local hydrology, ecosystems, and weather. The World Wide Web plugs individuals into an intercontinental cultural pulse from the big cities down to isolated villages and outposts, roiling traditional values and cultures. Supranational mechanisms of governance buck the prerogatives of sovereign states. Economic globalization drives and episodically disrupts national and local markets. The global poor, inundated with images of affluence, demand justice and seek access to wealthy countries, while despair, anger, and displacement feed the globalization of terrorism.

This scaling up of interconnection in the tangible space of institutions echoes in the subjective space of human consciousness. The nascent Planetary Phase elicits contradictory responses as some resist and others celebrate increasing interdependence. Antagonistic reaction to cosmopolitan intrusion has many faces: fundamentalism, nativism, isolationism, and anti-globalization. These powerful centrifugal forces could carry the day.

Still, even as the backlash swells and suppurates, an equally powerful centripetal force is at play: the enlargement of the human project presses for a corresponding enlargement of human identity. The intertwined destinies of people, generations, and all creatures stretch the arms of empathic embrace across space, time, and the natural world. The Planetary Phase has unleashed a mighty dialectic of chaos and order that drives, at once, toward splintered and integral futures. The fundamental quandary of the journey ahead is how to navigate these powerful cross-currents to a civilized Earthland.

Adumbrations

The Planetary Phase did not arrive unannounced. Tentacles of connectivity reach back to the early migrations out of Africa on humankind's long march to the ends of the earth. Through the millennia, human interchange reached across continents and oceans. Ancient trade routes carried people, products, and ideas over great distances; conquering empires encompassed much of the then-known world; and the great voyages of exploration wove the earliest strands of the web that would eventually entwine the whole planet.

These were the ancestral precursors, but the Planetary Phase is the direct child of the Modern Era. Modernity undercut the authority of received wisdom and the stasis of traditionalism, and put the pedal to the floor in the race to a world system. It injected the realm of thought with such radical concepts as progress, reason, democracy, individual rights, and the rule of law. It sparked revolutions in science and technology that powerfully enhanced human understanding of and mastery over nature. Capitalist economies, driven by the profit motive, liberated vast human potential for innovation and entrepreneurship, expanding production to unprecedented levels. The roar of the Industrial Revolution unleashed a previously unimaginable upsurge of acquisition and accumulation, growth and colonization.

For all the wealth created and ignorance defeated, the centuries of "creative destruction" have wrought untold human suffering and unprecedented environmental abuse. Capitalism's ineluctable expansion absorbed traditional societies at the edge of its retreating periphery into the nexus of market relations, or subdued them as colonies in empires of commerce. As the revolutions in science, religion, and society spread and gathered momentum, they encountered hard resistance at the moving frontier between modernist and traditionalist mindsets—still a jagged cultural fissure across the global field. Along a different fault line—the one between humanity and nature—the modern system, with its insatiable hunger for land and mineral resources, was cashing out nature's bounty. Eyes riveted on the bottom line were blind to the unaccounted costs accumulating off the books in the form of social impoverishment and ecological degradation.

As people and production filled the world, portents of the Planetary Phase arrived with greater frequency and intensity. The twentieth century opened with a surge of international trade, foreshadowing the mighty globalization at its close, but such trade soon became a casualty of the nationalistic inferno of two world wars. The United Nations rose on these embers to secure the peace for "we the people" (or so its visionary founders hoped), and the 1948 Universal Declaration of Human Rights sounded a clarion call for a supra-national ethos of dignity and liberty, entitlements of all people by virtue of their personhood alone.

Meanwhile, the exploitation of people and nature induced popular campaigns for justice and the environment, forerunners of contemporary civil society movements, but they could tame only the most egregious insults to the vulnerable and subordinate. Resistance to the maw of industrialism flared in the political and countercultural upsurges of the 1960s. A cosmopolitan spirit drew nourishment from the images transmitted by Apollo spacecraft of our borderless blue planet, a fragile jewel floating in endless darkness. All the while, though, the Cold War and the spread of nuclear weapons fed the awesome fear of global Armageddon.

By the 1980s, clear and insistent signals of a global shift were flashing across the spectrum of human affairs. Environmental concern arced out from the local to the global: from air and water pollution to the destabilization of the ecosphere. The drawdown of natural resources brought awareness of looming limits to oil, freshwater, and arable land. Mobile populations and the release of pathogens from fractured ecosystems brought fearsome epidemics. New communication technologies linked people and organizations in a latticework that globalized both goods and bads—social networks and criminal rings, economic development and financial volatility, research collaboration and cyberterrorism. On another front, the Soviet Union and kindred experiments elsewhere, asphyxiated by bureaucracy and shamed by the Gulag, squandered twentieth-century dreams of democratic socialist alternatives.

Capitalism's march toward world hegemony would not be denied. In the halls of power and academe, triumphant celebrants declared "the end of history," the world having reached a system for which, Margaret Thatcher proclaimed TINA, "there is no alternative." (In the streets, though, protesters insisted "another world is possible.") At the close of the twentieth century, market exuberance permeated the atmosphere. The rich were getting richer and proliferating in expanding pockets of wealth in the Global South; the wiring of the world promised a greater cornucopia to come; and corporations galloped the earth molding a globalized economy in their image. All the while, acute, concurrent crises were germinating that would surface in the new millennium to debunk neoliberal illusions.

In this century, we confront an unprecedented moment of uncertainty and opportunity. Rapid-fire, far-flung developments ripple across space and linger over time, altering the very coordinates of history. The quickening pace of change binds the future more tightly to the present; the gravitational pull of connectivity shrinks social space, pulling distant places and people into the orbit of an integrated world system. Most profoundly, the Planetary Phase nurtures awareness of the interdependence of generations and species, along with the local and global. The world-as-a-whole becomes a primary arena for the contending forms of consciousness that will determine whether the Planetary Phase will be an era of social evolution or devolution, environmental restoration or degradation.

This globalized configuration by no means abolishes communities and nations, which endure as vital loci of identity and engagement. Rather, Earthland forms an outer circle, a de facto global place if not yet a de jure "country," the site of great unfolding cultural and political struggles. Even as some countries have yet to undergo their modern revolution, history is moving at warp speed beyond modernity. The Planetary Phase has arrived as a discernible historical phenomenon.

Planetary Phase Ascending

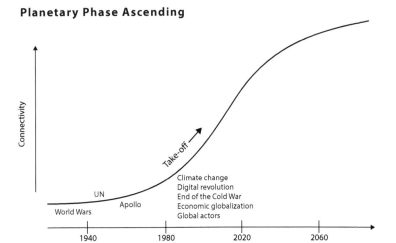

In any age, the ephemera of passing affairs obscure from view deep, slow-moving historical developments. In our time, incessant pings and distractions make perceiving the Big Story of our moment particularly difficult. But imagine a newspaper—call it *The Long Times*—that published only at great intervals, say, every half-century. Only the most sweeping news would appear above the fold, while daily headlines that once seemed consequential would be confined to its back pages, or become the forgotten minutiae of history. Arguably, the banner headline for the millennial edition might be: *World Enters the Planetary Phase of Civilization*. The question that animates this inquiry: What might be the lead story of the 2050 edition?

A turbulent time

What kind of country is Earthland today? An astute visitor, come to take the measure of the young nation, would find much to praise:

magnificent natural beauty and bounty; a colossal economy transmuting mountains of resources into rivers of products flowing nonstop to her four corners; extraordinary scientific achievements; and rich, diverse cultures. However, candor would compel this latter day Alexis de Tocqueville, having chronicled these assets, to catalog as well a daunting inventory of liabilities.

One cardinal defect would top the list: Earthland confronts twenty-first-century challenges hobbled by twentieth-century ideas and institutions. Zombie ideologies—territorial chauvinism, unbridled consumerism, and the illusion of endless growth—inhabit the brains of the living. Coherent responses to systemic risks of climate change, economic instability, population displacement, and global terrorism, to name only the most emblematic, lie beyond the grasp of a myopic and disputatious political order.

The disjuncture between old ways and new realities threatens the planetary commonweal, even the very continuity of civilization. A stable, flourishing Earthland, as with any country, depends on effectual governance supported by an informed polity. This foundation has not yet been laid. The consequences—rampant poverty, degradation of nature, hostile factions, absence of a legitimate constitutional authority—conjure images of other headless, dysfunctional countries. For now, Earthland resembles a failed state.

The resulting assaults on the tendrils of amity are many. A dog-eat-dog economy generates class chasms and lays nature to waste, undermining social cohesion and the integrity of the biosphere. The long tentacles of Hollywood and Madison Avenue spread unobtainable images of opulence, roiling traditional cultures and fanning hostility.

Displaced masses move toward centers of affluence where xenophobes stoke a protectionist backlash. The Internet serves as a planetary mall lubricating consumerism, and as a crime scene where malefactors ply nefarious trades. The geopolitical struggle for control of diminishing natural resources intensifies as growing economies demand ever-more energy, land, minerals, and water.

The scandalous income inequality in Earthland makes a country like Brazil, an epitome of social disparity, seem relatively egalitarian. At the bottom of the economic pyramid, 800 million people live mired in chronic hunger, with 161 million children stunted as a result. Nearly half the world's population subsists on less than $5 per day, the minimum reasonable income for an adequate standard of living. At the top, the richest 1% commands as much wealth as the other 99% combined—and the top 62 billionaires are as rich as the bottom 50%.[4]

The transformation of the earth itself enacts Earthland's most vivid crisis. The iconic issue is climate change, with its "inconvenient truths": the great danger of disruptive impacts, the need for massive and rapid action, and the unprecedented international cooperation required. Another is the impoverishment of biological resources—ecosystems, habitats, species—victims of land conversion, over-exploitation, and, increasingly, climate change. Toxification, the expanding brew of chemical pollutants injected into the environment, poses a third major threat. When we were Lilliputians on a vast planet, a civilization that ravaged its environment endangered only itself. Today, we are giants in planet-sized boots trampling the land, plundering the sea, and altering the chemistry of the biosphere.

Much attention has focused on each of these and myriad other global ills, much less on the systemic disruption that underlies and links them. To adapt a venerable parable, experts illuminate various parts of the global elephant, but fail to apprehend the whole beast. The knowledge they generate on leg, tail, and trunk does not sum to the pachyderm. Correspondingly, partial and anodyne policy prescriptions may salve this or that symptom of the disease, but they leave the underlying pathology to fester.

The Planetary Phase, born of systemic crisis, urges a systemic response. Feedbacks are everywhere: environmental stress exacerbates poverty and incites conflict, thereby threatening economic stability; economic instability weakens efforts to protect nature and reduce poverty; desperate underclasses degrade the environment and seek access to affluent countries, exciting backlash that undercuts geo-economic cooperation. The mounting pressure embrittles the structure of the whole social-ecological system as its resilience—the capacity to recover from a disturbance—becomes compromised.

Under these increasingly vulnerable conditions, various triggers could induce a general, system-wide crisis. To wit, *abrupt climate change* could generate food shortages, economic instability, mass migration, and conflict. A *pandemic*, spread by the mobile affluent and uprooted poor, could ripple far and wide, overwhelming healthcare institutions. The mayhem induced by a *macro-terrorist attack* could segue into a degenerative cycle of violence and disorder. Absolute *shortage of vital resources*, such as water, oil, and arable land, could generate a tsunami of chaos. A *collapse of the global financial system* could ignite a cascade of knock-on disruption.[5]

The world has become one interconnected place, but not yet one integral nation. Years of denial and drift have allowed the preconditions for cataclysm to strengthen. Still, it is not too late to turn toward system-wide solutions. An abundance of means are available for muting common risks and pursuing common goals, and new innovations are reported daily. But bending the curve of development toward a flourishing civilization will take a Great Transition from a world of strangers to a commonwealth of citizens. This worthier outcome, latent in the evolving historical matrix, awaits bold vision and collective action to bring it forth.

Tomorrowlands

Branching scenarios

Whither Earthland? The only certainty about the future is surprise, the one constant change: indeterminacy and dynamism are woven into the fabric of reality from quantum to global scales. Complex systems of many stripes can cross critical thresholds of instability where old structures crumble and new structures form, with the outcome inherently uncertain and sensitive to small deflections.

In particular, social evolution, a highly complex process, twists and turns through a tangled tree of possibilities, where major branching points mark the transformation from one epoch to another. The form of the successor society is not predetermined—nor is it unrestricted. As Marx quipped, people make their own history, but not as they please. Historical necessity curbs human freedom, while the interplay of intention and circumstance loosens the grip of necessity, opening a bandwidth of possible futures. The path actually taken becomes etched onto the timeline of history, while the foregone alternatives are lost to memory, or serve as fodder for the "what-if" scenarios of counterfactual histories.

Thus, predicting the ultimate shape of the twenty-first-century world is a fool's errand. The destiny of our no-analog century lies beyond the ken of scientific projection and social prophecy. Although the conceit of prediction must be abandoned, we still can explore alternative possibilities, not to forecast what will be, but to envision what could be. Scenarios are prostheses for the imagination, giving breadth and specificity to our longer-term outlooks. Rich visions, when they influence consciousness and action, inject a teleological dimension into the dynamics of social change, drawing history toward desirable outcomes.[6]

A simple "taxonomy of the future" helps organize the branching menagerie of possibilities. At the highest level, three broad channels fan out from the unsettled present into the imagined future: worlds of incremental adjustment (*Conventional Worlds*), worlds of calamitous discontinuity (*Barbarization*), and worlds of progressive transformation (*Great Transitions*). This archetypal triad—evolution, decline, and progression—recurs throughout the history of ideas, finding new expression in the contemporary scenario literature. To add texture, we expand the typology with two variations for each category, as indicated in the following figure.[7]

Taxonomy of the Future

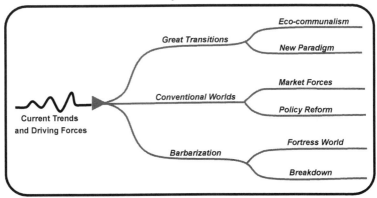

Conventional Worlds evolve without a fundamental shift in the prevailing social paradigm or structure of the world system. Episodic setbacks notwithstanding, persistent tendencies—corporate globalization, the spread of dominant values, and poor-country emulation of rich-country production and consumption patterns—drive the regnant model forward. Needless to say, we could spin endless variations on this theme by adjusting technological, environmental, and geopolitical assumptions, among many other variables. To underscore a central ideological divide within the mainstream discourse, we highlight two subclasses within Conventional Worlds. *Market Forces* variants envision globalized free markets and deregulation as paramount drivers of development. By contrast, *Policy Reform* variants, rooted in social democratic rather than neoliberal sensibilities, feature comprehensive, coordinated government actions to rewire modern capitalism in order to alleviate poverty and spare the environment.

However, all the while, Barbarization scenarios, the evil cousins of Conventional Worlds, lurk, feeding on unattended crises. In these dark visions, a deluge of instability—social polarization, geopolitical conflict, environmental degradation, economic failure, and the rampaging macro-crisis of climate change—swamps the corrective mechanisms of free markets and government policy. A systemic global crisis thereby spirals out of control as civilized norms dissolve. Barbarized futures, too, could take many forms (enough to inspire multitudinous apocalyptic novels and screenplays), but two idealized types—*Fortress Worlds* and *Breakdown*—capture the main lines. In Fortress Worlds variants, elites retreat to protected enclaves, leaving an impoverished majority outside, as powerful global forces mobilize to impose order and environmental controls. In Breakdown variants, such a coherent authoritarian intervention fails to materialize (or proves inadequate), chaos intensifies, and institutions collapse. A new Dark Age descends.

Great Transitions imagine how the powerful exigencies and novel opportunities of the Planetary Phase might advance more enlightened aspirations. An ascendant suite of values—human solidarity, quality of life, and an ecological sensibility—counters the conventional triad of individualism, consumerism, and domination of nature. This shift in consciousness underpins a corresponding shift in institutions, toward democratic global governance, economies geared to the well-being of all, and sound environmental stewardship. Two kinds of Great Transition scenarios—*Eco-communalism* and *New Paradigm*—highlight a key distinction within the contemporary radical imagination.

Eco-communalism reflects the ardent localism that is a strong philosophical and political current within environmental, social justice, and anti-globalization subcultures. Certainly, the vision it champions of autarkic communities and small-scale enterprises guided by face-to-face democracy will remain a vital element in any Great Transition project. (Indeed, it is a prominent element in the "destination" we imagine for Earthland in Part III.) But so must the cosmopolitan sensibility that welcomes global identity and citizenship as desirable and necessary: the foundation for a true planetary civilization and a counterforce to parochial bigotries. At any rate, in an increasingly interdependent world, it is difficult to identify a plausible path to a thoroughgoing Eco-communal Earthland, except perhaps via one that first passes through the shattered world of Breakdown.

The New Paradigm—the Great Transition vision embraced in this essay—imagines a world at once plural and unified. It rejects the false polarity of bottom-up communalism and top-down hierarchy, inviting a search for ways to reconcile and balance them. It thus celebrates flourishing places in a nested system of communities from the local to the global, while nourishing a world polity as a surrounding layer of community and identity. Rather than retreat to radical localism, this kind of Great Transition seeks to reshape and guide the character of planetary civilization. Utopian no more, this vision has become anchored in the objective conditions of history: the intertwined destinies of people and Earth.

Dramatis personae

While well-told tales of the future in the form of religious eschatology or speculative fiction may inspire or transfix, compelling real-world scenarios must persuade. Simulation models help illuminate the *technical plausibility* of different scenarios by evaluating the realism of their assumed socioeconomic patterns in light of resource and environmental constraints, a taxing but relatively straightforward analytic exercise. Making a tenable case for *social plausibility* is the less tractable challenge, requiring a portrayal of a "history of the future" that is consistent with the emerging dynamics of society and with "the crooked timber of humanity" out of which, said Kant, no straight thing was ever made.

A key step is identifying a scenario's agents of change: the dramatis personae who could plausibly drive its narrative forward.[8] Some leading protagonists are already at center stage, while others gather in the wings. The leading characters of Market Forces—transnational corporations and their political allies—have been the familiar players driving the first phase of corporate-driven globalization. The clout of these behemoths has grown hand-in-hand with the borderless economy, the largest companies becoming more powerful economic actors than many countries.[9] Without plan or blueprint, a complex architecture of production circuits, labor markets, and capital flows rises as an aggregation structure built on the countless actions of footloose enterprises. Corporate actors pursuing profit in a planetary emporium and applying vast resources to secure compliant decision-makers would continue to orient development in a Market Forces world.

In Policy Reform stories, rejuvenated governments play the leading role, vigorously rectifying the instabilities induced by over-reliance on market mechanisms. Globally synchronized regulations, incentives, and agreements constrain capitalism and steer development toward an array of environmental and social sustainability goals. The United Nations becomes the multilateral hub for formulating and implementing this New Global Deal. A second critical actor, civil society—a vast polyglot of organizations and campaigns—presses government action on the full spectrum of issues through education and lobbying, and protests when called for.

The Fortress World scenario features a new global alliance—military organizations, trade bodies, planning units, multilateral associations—at the heart of a global authoritarian regime that imposes harsh order in close collaboration with big business. In a Breakdown scenario, divisive legions—jingoistic nationalists, criminal networks plying the global bazaar, militant fundamentalists, and purveyors of atavistic ideologies and murderous activity—multiply in the interstices of global society, feeding on its conflicts and crises. They bring down the curtain on civilization, at least for a time.

None of the principal characters now on the global stage are strong candidates to be trailblazers of a Great Transition. In different ways, they express concerns too narrow and outlooks too myopic for the task. Thus, the United Nations, relying on the cooperation of its reluctant member countries, ardent defenders of their own national interests, cannot mount an adequate response to the crisis and promise of the Planetary Phase; the top priority for corporations remains higher returns for shareholders, not the common good; and institutionalized civil society organizations, plowing their separate vineyards and competing for donor funds, are ill-prepared for the larger project of conceptualizing and advancing a coherent system shift.

Movements for "personal transformation" offer an escapist and depoliticizing alternative for those dispirited by this leadership vacuum. According to some New Age teachers, the individual pursuit of meaning and solace through psychological and metaphysical practices can change for the better, not only our lives, but the world we live in. Indeed, alternate paths to fulfillment and spiritual peace are essential for countering the hegemony of materialism. However, the personal and political cannot be disentangled, and the search for private answers alone cannot without engagement and action lead to collective solutions.

Who speaks for Earthland?

We can hardly expect the entrenched institutions of the current order—corporations, governments, large civil society organizations—to be at the forefront of efforts to supersede it. With deep stakes in maintaining the status quo, they are too timorous and too venal to address profound environmental and social problems. They would be as miscast for a revolutionary role as would have been the feudal aristocracy in leading the charge to modernity. We need to look elsewhere for a leading actor. History offers a clue.

In stable periods, societies change gradually within resilient boundaries of norms and values. Then, in periods when systemic crisis strikes and interrupts historical continuity, everything changes at once, and the scope for human choice and freedom expands. The interregnum, as the old society fades and before a new one solidifies, can be a time of great confusion, fear, and polarization. The crisis spawns counter-hegemonic groups, some of which may emerge to spearhead the consolidation of a new social formation. Indeed, when such revolutionary forces do not materialize, the spent society can collapse and vanish, as many have.

For example, the priestly and royal castes, the progenitors of the first civilizations, were the offspring of the early agricultural societies they supplanted. Much later, the entrepreneurial classes, the motive force of early capitalism, germinated in the mercantile crevices of the European feudal system they eventually buried. Nearer our own time, the socialist upheavals of the past two centuries expressed the egalitarian impulse of a working class aspiring to transcend the industrial system that created it. Perhaps the most salient forerunner to the contemporary challenge can be found in the popular movements that first forged nation-states. They arose as modernizing forces within the belly of archaic societies to superimpose national identities and institutions on preexisting communities.

Now it is we who live in the interregnum between a familiar world that was and a different one in the making. Is the crisis of modernity nurturing a protagonist capable of galvanizing the progressive potential of our epoch? The signature feature of the Planetary Phase—the enmeshment of all in an overarching proto-country—suggests an answer. As modernity once birthed national movements, the Planetary Phase clamors for a global movement: an encompassing cultural and political awakening united under the banner of Earthland.

Hence, the natural change agent for a Great Transition would be a *global citizens movement*, a vast cultural and political rising, able to redirect policy, tame corporations, and unify civil society. The contemporary world stage is missing this critical actor, but it is stirring on a planet bubbling with intensifying crises and shifting consciousness. A harbinger is the army of engaged people working on a thousand fronts for justice, peace, and sustainability.

For now though, without a systemic movement to unify and inspire, activists are left to address epiphenomena, rather than underlying causes. In the absence of a coherent strategy, systemic deterioration outpaces fragmentary gains. Exhausted and frustrated, many activists burn out, while many more concerned citizens never find a meaningful way to engage a crisis so amorphous and overwhelming. A global movement, were it to develop, would speak especially to this growing band of the disempowered: to their minds, with a unifying perspective; to their hearts, with a vision of a better world; and to their feet, with an organizational context for action.

The civil society upsurge of the past quarter century has paved the way for a more comprehensive oppositional configuration—and highlighted its necessity. It is time to comprehend the many problems we confront as manifestations of a unitary crisis and thereby understand the many struggles as separate tasks in a common project. We will consider the contours of a movement for Earthland and ways to nurture it later in this essay. First, though, the case needs to be made that "planetizing our movement" is no longer a pipe dream, but a propitious historical project.[10]

◇◇◇◇◇◇◇

PART II
PATHWAY: A SAFE PASSAGE

With its provenance in the twentieth century, Earthland swings toward its providence in the twenty-first. We are poised at the fulcrum, buffeted by menacing crosswinds, buoyed by wisps of hope. Grim prognoses abound as fear for the future globalizes along with everything else. But the future is not just some place we are going, grim or otherwise. It is a world we are creating—for worse, if despair disempowers the better angels of our nature, or for better, if we travelers awaken and together set course.

Peril in the mainstream

Is there a path to a flourishing civilization within a Conventional Worlds framework? When they proffer small-bore correctives, opinion shapers and decision-makers implicitly assume so. Whether they realize it or not, they are, in the name of prudence, gambling that mega-crises will not overwhelm gradual market and policy responses. Counting on institutional adaptation and structural continuity may be a good bet in the near term, but becomes an increasingly risky wager over a multi-decade time frame.

With the long-term path riddled with pitfalls and tipping points, Market Forces reliance on maximally free markets is an especially quixotic and therefore deeply irresponsible creed. True, the mighty engine of capitalism with its imperatives to accumulate and innovate has opened broad vistas for human progress and freedom (and, indeed, laid the historical foundation for a Great Transition). But capitalism's tendencies to exploit people, concentrate wealth, and lay waste to nature drive the contemporary crisis, and prescribing more of the same would only further bleed the patient. By sapping social-ecological resilience, this scenario, ironically, would negate the very "business-as-usual" premises—perpetual economic growth and institutional continuity—it holds dear. Rather than a path to market utopia, this unfettered course would more plausibly be a shortcut to Barbarization.

Recognizing these dangers, legions of reformers champion the reassertion of governance authority to tame corporate capitalism and steer it toward sustainability. For a quarter century, policymakers and analysts, spurred by civil society activists, have generated a veritable athenaeum of proposals for nudging the system with incentives, taxes, and regulations. The Policy Reform approach reached a rhetorical crescendo at the 1992 Earth Summit, but then faded in the torrent of globalization that followed. The recently adopted UN Post-2015 Development Agenda returns reform to the center of international discourse, although the Agenda's modest implementation commitments and business-almost-as-usual "green economy" framing may again clip the wings of its lofty goals.

Despite the best efforts of dedicated reform advocates, systemic deterioration has overwhelmed the piecemeal progress made to reorient the conventional paradigm. This reality disappoints but should not surprise or discourage, for these are the early days of counter-hegemonic ferment. Reform campaigns are needed more than ever to ease human suffering, slow the pace of destruction, and spread awareness. But their limited success does reinforce concern that, tacking against the mighty winds of a dysfunctional system, reform can take us only so far.

A Policy Reform approach to shaping Earthland, if implemented rapidly and thoroughly, would be technically feasible. Studies show that there are massive technological and policy means at the ready—and new innovations reported daily—to eradicate poverty, close income gaps, and avert environmental catastrophe.[11] In principle, at least, a full-scale Policy Reform mobilization could bend the curve of history toward a just and sustainable future. The good news is technical feasibility; the bad news is political infeasibility. Radically altering production and consumption practices within a conventional framework would be akin to trying to climb up a down escalator. Rather than helping, the machinery—profit motive, corporate power, consumerist values, state-centric politics—pushes in the opposite direction.

The drive to accumulate and expand is embedded in the very DNA of capitalism, at once the system's genius and Achilles heel. Prodded by competition, profit-seeking entrepreneurs seek new markets, modernize production processes, and devise new commodities, amplifying sales through design allure and advertising guile. The financial sector amps the growth machine. Governments work to maintain the vitality of the commercial sphere and, when crises strike, bail out the too-big-to-fail. On the demand side, consumer capitalism cultivates the worship of Mammon and the mania for "stuff." On the hedonic treadmill, lubricated by the creation of needs and wants through sophisticated marketing techniques, possessions become the measure of individual identity and social status.

A step-by-step ascension against this push-back would take tenacious leadership and unprecedented international cooperation. Where would the necessary political will come from? It is nowhere in sight, not surprising in a political culture that takes economic growth as the barometer of social progress and associates material consumption with the good life, and where the sacrosanct principle of nation-state sovereignty stifles wider cooperation. A coherent telling of the Policy Reform scenario must account for the elevation of political leadership courageous and strong enough to counter all this resistance. Conceivably, if social forces from within the establishment and from the popular base surge and converge, the political foundation for a New Global Deal might be forged. The "retrospective" sketch below imagines how history might turn toward Policy Reform.

Policy Reform: A Retrospective

Shanghai, 2084

A century ago, a perfect storm gathered that was to irrevocably alter the world system. A gale of economic globalization, technological innovation, and environmental change signaled the onset of a new historical phase. Multinational corporations and banks spun long chains of production and finance, while new-money arrivistes swelled the demand side of the economic equation. As the Cold War receded, the "Washington Consensus" mantra—free trade, deregulation, modernization—echoed through the halls of power.

This rapturous late twentieth-century interlude, with its fragile arrangements and bogus ideology, could not endure. The snowballing crisis that arrived with the new millennium (inaugurating the historical period now referred to as the Rolling Crisis) sobered all but those most intoxicated with free market euphoria. Nevertheless, corporate-driven globalization sputtered along on a collision course with the hard facts of a finite biosphere and a polarized world. Public denial and private self-interest reinforced the enormous inertia built into the conventional system, long delaying widespread mobilization to address social-ecological risks.

As the world convulsed with violence, war, and privation, voices for change stirred in two major arenas. From above, enlightened elites, recognizing the existential threat to the market system itself, advocated taming capitalism for its own good. From below, civil society campaigns and people's movements organized cadres of citizens frustrated with the ineptitude of government and ready to take action. As masses clamored for fundamental change, establishment reformists, fearing a revolutionary upsurge, sought a "third way." The New Global Deal they rallied around included comprehensive institutional change and policy action to improve economic equity and strengthen ecological resilience in their many dimensions.

The reform discourse, with roots in the 1972 UN Stockholm Conference on the Human Environment, continued through the decades of international meetings that followed. Eloquent declarations articulated noble aspirations, but action failed to match rhetoric: weak international bodies could not counter the defenders of the status quo. The balance began to shift, however, with the UN's Post-2015 Development Agenda. The centerpiece was a set of Sustainable

Development Goals that included a wide array of environmental and social indicators and targets. At first, the SDGs seemed destined to become another toothless edict, lacking the political commitment and financial resources needed to convert good intentions into facts on the ground. However, each jolt of the Rolling Crisis galvanized reformers and brought forth new leaders. Most importantly, it stirred popular movements demanding that the promise of 2015 be fulfilled.

This cultural and political awakening—often referred to as the "global citizens movement" (GCM)—played a crucial role. With its genesis in civil society activism, the movement channeled the public's growing impatience with leaders unwilling or unable to act forcefully. In the 2020s, networks of NGOs, local activists, and people's movements spread and strengthened, creatively utilizing the Internet as a forum and coordinating space, and as a commons to foster a sense of global community. Riding a wave of collective discontent and reawakened hope, a growing chorus clamored for action. The GCM sprang up in ubiquitous nodes tailored to local places and specific issues, yet attuned to planetary concerns and opportunities. The Global Spring had sprung.

In the context of this popular ferment, the reformist coalition strengthened, enlisting forward-looking governments, corporations, and NGOs. The resistance from the old guard of special interests and political reactionaries grew fierce. This motley band branded the reformers as planetary socialists, while the extreme left disparaged them as corporate lackeys, but the centrist faction gained traction nevertheless. As the crisis intensified, its slogan—"Modernize or Barbarize"— came to seem less alarmist hyperbole and more a stark choice. The surging GCM signed on, aiding the rapid ascent of progressive leaders and political parties.

The sea change of reform altered political cultures almost everywhere. The UN was reorganized and streamlined to serve as a potent twenty-first-century coordinating authority. Wealthy countries reduced their environmental footprints and assisted poorer countries in leapfrogging to sustainable forms of development. Progress was monitored carefully and targets adjusted periodically in response to changing trends and new scientific knowledge. Gradually, Earthland was becoming a global social democracy—too gradually for the restless activists of the revitalized GCM. But that is another story….

If, in contrast to the successful reform scenario sketched above, contradictions in the mainstream prove politically insuperable amidst destabilizing perils, established institutions would lose legitimacy and coherence. Then, absent strong countervailing social movements, conditions would favor a historical swerve toward Barbarization. It is a disheartening but hardly surprising sign of our times that many observers believe that the true "business-as-usual" scenario veers from familiar Conventional Worlds territory into a dystopian landscape. Indeed, it takes little more than a mathematical bent and a limited imagination to confidently extrapolate from current trends to descent into a doleful future.

Barbarization tales begin—as all scenarios must—in the here and now: a world rife with crisis and contention. Warning bells sound with ever greater frequency and urgency but, nonetheless, the forces of correction—government programs, civil society activism, popular movements—remain weak, and instability spreads. In Fortress World versions of the story of descent, a powerful global alliance acts to impose order in the face of looming chaos. The revolution-from-above establishes an autocratic global authority that persists for many years. Eventually, though, a general uprising of the excluded could signal the resumption of the long-delayed Great Transition project. At least this seems to be the hope of our correspondent in her dispatch below from a Fortress World.

Fortress World: Looking Back and Ahead

Free Zone, 2084

At the onset of the Planetary Phase, sleepwalking elites failed to confront the tectonic disruptions underway. In fairness, the best of them did sound the alert and work tirelessly to rectify the situation, but could wrench only feeble corrections from a hidebound system. The zenith of this Policy Reform tendency was the hodgepodge of laudable aspirations in the so-called UN Post-2015 Development Agenda, but the agreement did not address the deep drivers of social-ecological instability and inequity. Predictably, the political and financial commitment to "sustainable development goals" soon waned, and dangerous trends marched on. The high rhetoric of 2015 became the eulogy for the lost era of sustainability.

The Rolling Crisis, which was in full throttle by the mid-2020s, eroded social stability and spread a corrosive zeitgeist of suspicion and despair. As mayhem mounted, only die-hard neoliberals and aging economists clung to discredited dreams of capitalist utopia. Progressives still proposed and protested, but with diminishing conviction. A movement for a Great Transition surged briefly then dissipated, enfeebled by ideological incoherence and strategic fragmentation. The leadership vacuum became a breeding ground for nihilism, survivalism, and paranoia.

The global economy grew slowly, but benefited only the 1%. A supranational affluent class coalesced, bound by common interests and worldviews. The excluded masses grew more wretched, alienated, and angry. International aid, never sufficient, became miserly as priorities turned to security and crisis management. Tantalized by images of opulence and opportunity in the rich enclaves, desperate billions sought access by any means necessary. Some found sanctuary and second-class citizenship; most were greeted by high walls and virulent xenophobia.

Meanwhile, jolts of systemic dysfunction—climate disasters, sectarian conflict, horrific terrorism, merciless pandemics, food shortages, and all the rest—hit more frequently and severely. The chaos was a godsend for criminal syndicates, terrorist networks, and corrupt officials extracting scarce lucre from the body politic. The anarchy inflamed ethnic, religious, and nationalist hostilities, reaching a nadir with the nuclear exchange in South Asia. The collapse of civil order threatened to engulf even the privileged.

As the world system hemorrhaged, the so-called *NEO* alliance took forceful action, anointing itself a provisional world authority, and acted with military precision to impose its self-styled *New Earth Order*. The NEO movement began as an international forum on the global problematique, where the masters of the universe—corporate leaders, powerful politicians, thought leaders— deliberated and built networks. Initially innocuous, the talk shop metamorphosed rapidly as the general crisis descended, becoming a coordinating body for international action. Some participants were philosophically reluctant to take the draconian step of asserting authoritarian control, but by the mid-2030s, the TINA ("there is no alternative") faction carried the day. The NEO putsch met with pockets of opposition, but organized resistance collapsed in disarray as a planet-wide state of emergency was declared and civil rights suspended. The authorities unified national militaries of the willing into a "peace brigade" to enforce their cynical "3S" program: Stability, Security, and Sustainability. Using the revamped UN as a coordinating platform and legal cover, the NEO forces swept through hot spots, launching sporadic shock and awe attacks. Relying on big data and sophisticated surveillance, harsh police measures quelled conflict and suppressed dissent, while protecting vital natural resources for the new power elite.

The New Earth Order (or *Global Apartheid* to its detractors) codified the separate spheres of haves and have-nots in asymmetrical legal and institutional frameworks. The affluent flourished in their archipelago of protected islands— bubbles of privilege in an ocean of misery. In the police state outside, the majority were mired in poverty and denied basic freedoms. The Fortress World era has persisted for nearly a half-century, suppressing the waves of organized resistance that heroically formed in the interstices of the beast. Now, though, as the cry "Enough!" rises in the liberated zones and throughout this restless world, its days may be numbered. On the horizon, the phoenix of hope awakens and spreads its wings.

Can a Conventional Worlds path avoid an oppressive future like that sketched in this dispatch? Moreover, can such a path lead to a flourishing civilization? The judicious answer is that the odds of success are long and that failure would be potentially catastrophic. To maintain otherwise is to ignore, deny, or sugarcoat the contradictions between the dynamics of the standard paradigm and the requirements of the Planetary Phase. The accumulation of wealth concentrates power and influence, while consumerism, polarization, and individualism constrain collective action. Short-termism keeps politicians focused on the next election, not the next generation; profit trumps people and the environment; and nationalism subverts common action.

In immoderate times, moderation becomes imprudent—madness in reason's mask. The business-as-usual utopianism of Market Forces ideology is an egregious case of crackpot realism (to borrow a phrase from C. Wright Mills). Level-headed reformers at least recognize the dangers, but embrace a utopian hope of their own: namely, that sufficient political will can materialize to adequately quell perilous trends without fundamentally altering human values and social institutions. No doubt, Policy Reform efforts will remain an essential near-term prong of a Great Transition strategic thrust, but alone carry the danger of diverting attention and resources from the longer-term task of root-and-branch rectification. Meanwhile, the unrelenting gears of Market Forces grind on.

A scenario can be problematic in two ways: as *description*, when analysis suggests it is technically or socially infeasible, and as *prescription*, when it clashes with human aspirations and is deemed undesirable. So far, our critique of Conventional Worlds scenarios has focused on the former: their realism and viability as descriptions of the future. But let us suspend disbelief for just a moment and assume that a conventional future is feasible. The prescriptive question would remain: Would these paths lead to a desirable civilization? Or would the world instead come to resemble a well-engineered mall in which the environment continues to deliver essential services and few people starve, but not a place where people flourish and nature thrives?

To recoil at truncated Conventional Worlds visions is to add a normative dimension to the instrumental critique of the dominant paradigm. Along the centrist path, astute and idealistic travelers to Earthland confront a thorny twofold question: Can we get there, and would we want to live there? They search for persuasive and comforting answers, but finding only dubious means and lamentable ends, turn to seek a better way.

Triads of transformation

A double force—the push of necessity and the pull of desire—propels a Great Transition. The pressing need to prevent an impoverished future animates our reformist instincts, but reform alone lacks potency and inspiration. The lure of an enriched future excites our inner revolutionist, but relying on vision alone leaves us whistling past the graveyard. Amelioration and transformation are the flip sides of one strategic coin for moving toward a viable and worthy planetary civilization.

Visions of Earthland serve as a social compass orienting the journey in the right general direction, not as a roadmap through the thicket of danger and uncertainty that lies in the *terra incognita* ahead.

The travelers have no choice but to forge the path en route, learning the lay of the land and correcting course, eyes kept firmly on the prize. They embark on a voyage of discovery with no guarantee of reaching a desirable future world. But the promise is real, and the search itself exhilarating.

Critics are not sold. The most skeptical denigrate the enterprise as a utopian dream (or dangerous folly). These naysayers may lack social imagination, but their implicit question—Is a Great Transition attainable?—deserves a persuasive response. After all, the vision is bold, and even constricted Conventional Worlds visions tax credulity, albeit for very different reasons. For the Great Transition scenario to gain adherents, its central premise—that a cultural and political awakening can bring forth a flourishing planetary civilization—must be seen as at least plausible. Then, even if pessimistic about the *probabilities*, we can, like Lewis Mumford, be optimistic about the *possibilities*.

The case for plausibility rests on our reading of the historical moment. The pivot toward the Planetary Phase brings a negation of what is and an affirmation of what could be. On the one hand, the burgeoning crisis of modernity delegitimizes the current system; on the other, embryonic conditions nurture the germ of a more civilized system. The erosion of faith in orthodox approaches opens psychic and political space for envisioning radically different alternatives, but disenchantment taken alone can breed demagoguery and presage social retrogression. Hope lies with the affirmative developments that objectively and subjectively make a Great Transition possible.

What are such developments? For one, the material foundations now exist: the spectacular productive capacity of the contemporary world economy could underwrite an equitable, post-scarcity world. Of equal significance, a host of shared risks begging for forceful supranational cooperation has put the idea and practice of planetary governance on the historic agenda. Interdependence in the objective realm of political economy cultivates, in the subjective realm of human consciousness, an understanding of people and planet as a single community. The intertwining of fates urges a new cosmopolitanism that welcomes the unity of a global demos and the diversity of cultures and places—and pushes beyond species solidarity to solidarity with fellow creatures and all planetary forms of being.

Every age generates a constellation of values coherent with its social arrangements. The modernist ethos once rose in concert with incipient exigencies but has now become out of sync with twenty-first-century realities. Modernity's canon of perpetual progress gains little purchase in a time of thwarted expectations and existential apprehension. An international order based on the Westphalian model of inviolable state sovereignty clashes with global interdependence and the very idea of Earthland. The destabilization of the biosphere debunks the idolatry of markets, the myth of perpetual economic growth, and the fetish of consumerism. Corrosive inequality and hollowed-out communities sap allegiance to dog-eat-dog capitalism.

The lacuna between old verities and new realities, already dangerous, will widen along the current historical trajectory. Ameliorative policies can soften the contradictions and tweak the direction, not ensure safe passage to a decent destination. That will take fundamental changes in both human consciousness and the social model: the inner "normative realm" and the outer "institutional realm." As the following figure suggests, these modes would coevolve in a systemic shift: nascent values drive institutional change; new institutions imprint values into social practice. Thus, efforts to nurture holistic values and social change struggles, the central prongs of an integrated strategy, are dialectically linked and mutually reinforcing.

The Three-Fold Way of Transition

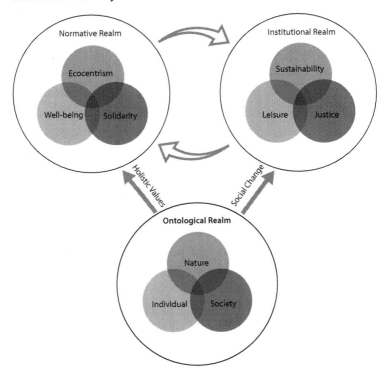

The triad of Great Transition values shown in the normative realm applies to vastly different domains of the "ontological realm"

(see figure). Well-being centers on the *individual*, solidarity on the *human species*, and ecocentrism on the *biosphere*. Although they address disparate dimensions of the human experience, these values share a common theme: the longing for wholeness. The desire for defragmented lives, societies, and ecosystems anchors the social vision and guides efforts to shape the institutional realm. Human fulfillment, social equity, and environmental sustainability, afterthoughts in Conventional Worlds, become the cornerstones of the good society. These normative desiderata are the foundation for creating institutions that provide the time and resources for the pursuit of fulfilling lives, ensure social and economic justice, foster citizen engagement and democratic governance, and strengthen the resilience and biodiversity of the natural environment.

Economic design in particular has cross-cutting significance because it mediates our relationship to nature and to each other. Great Transition economies would be understood as the proximate means to the ultimate ends of vibrant lives, harmonious societies, qualitative, not quantitative, development. Innovation would continue in a post-material-growth era—indeed, would likely soar. But these new economies, by whatever name, would be post-capitalist, since private profit and capital accumulation would no longer have primacy. Some places might rely on governmental controls, others on decentralized arrangements, and still others on social ownership and workers control. Part III of this essay envisions how various economic approaches could coexist in post-transition Earthland.

The three-fold way of change encompasses an immense spectrum of cultural and political efforts. Already, movements and organizations are working on numerous fronts to educate, inspire, and reform. The concern for quality of life finds expression in indigenous communities struggling to retain their ways of life as well as the many affluent subcultures seeking to withdraw from frenetic consumer capitalism in order to cultivate "sharing economies," local community, and the art of living. The spirit of solidarity manifests in struggles for universal rights, poverty eradication, and democratic global governance. The ecological sensibility animates innumerable efforts to restructure patterns of production and consumption for fitness with natural processes.

This explosion of oppositional energy and alternative practice could foreshadow a systemic and affirmative awakening, but for now remains too fragmented and too reactive. A mature movement for a Great Transition would bring multifarious initiatives and campaigns under a broad umbrella of common concerns: What constitutes the good life? How shall we organize society? What should be our relationship to the natural world? Learning how to weave the many strands into a synergistic planetary praxis stands as the most critical challenge on the journey to Earthland. We will explore ways to do so after first establishing the technical feasibility of a Great Transition.

Through-lines

If there is a will, there is a way—a plethora of ways—to deflect, reverse, and supersede ominous trends. Even within the constrictive ideological confines of a Policy Reform scenario, massive technological and policy means could be deployed, in principle, to gradually bend curves of peril away from calamity. However, the curves would bend farther and faster in a Great Transition, which would both disable the sources of pernicious social-ecological pressures and expand the universe of policy options. To explore the technical potential, let us assume for a moment that transformative cultural and political predicates develop in the coming decades: a vast civic upsurge gains momentum in constraining corporations, reining in power structures, propagating social enterprises, and bringing a new generation of leaders committed to the new agenda.

In this context, recalibrated institutions and incentive structures would spur innovation and uptake of green technology, while strong redistributive policies would rapidly reduce inequality and poverty. In so doing, a Great Transition scenario might superficially seem to resemble a Policy Reform scenario on steroids. However, potent social shifts—post-capitalist economies, low-impact lifestyles, and paths to modernization in poor countries that leapfrog the resource-intensive industrial model—would add powerful levers of change unavailable in conventional scenarios. As a result, social and environmental patterns would peel away sharply from trend lines as the world system veers toward a different configuration for Earthland. To illustrate the possibilities, the following paragraphs, drawing from detailed computer simulations, compare Great Transition (GT) and Market Forces (MF) outlooks for selected indicators.[12]

World population, currently about 7.5 billion people, is projected to increase by perhaps three billion in the course of this century, nearly all in poorer countries.[13] Under GT conditions, by contrast, the proto-country of Earthland undergoes a demographic shift to lower birth and death rates, not unlike that previously experienced in affluent countries as they industrialized and modernized. Rapid social progress on a number of fronts—education, health, family planning, and career opportunity—liberates and empowers women, leading to changing family structures and reduced fertility rates. Under these conditions, world

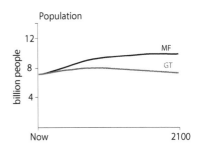

population peaks in mid-century, and then gradually declines.

What about the economic picture? The scale of the GT global economy would be substantially lower than typical projections. One major factor accounting for the difference is that immense non-productive expenditures—military armaments, advertising, and a host of other wasteful activities—are wrung from the economy. Most significantly, productivity gains (output per hour of work), instead of increasing aggregate economic output, are used to decrease socially necessary labor,

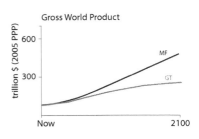

as consumerism fades and demand for leisure time grows.

Rising economic security, along with more equitable income and wealth distributions, sets the context for the shift in economic priorities. As livelihoods become reliable and sufficient in a GT world, people grow more concerned with the quality of life in its many dimensions: relationships, community, creativity, recreation, and spiritual fulfillment. The growing preference for "rich lives, not lives of riches" is reflected in shorter workweeks (and years of work) and correspondingly greater discretionary time. But this by no means implies that Earthland would be a land of ascetics: its average income of about $30,000

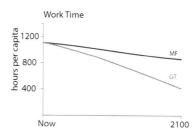

per person at the end of the century would be comparable to Italy today. All would enjoy secure and comfortable standards of living as the foundation for pursuit of non-materialistic satisfactions.

How might the fight against the scourge of poverty fare in one future versus another? Human destitution remains a stubborn feature of a Market Forces future. Aggregate economic growth would reduce world poverty, but increases in population and inequality would partially negate the gains, leaving hundreds of millions still mired in chronic hunger. By contrast, a Great Transition, focused on human well-being and economic security, makes poverty elimination a galvanizing priority. A constellation of factors contributes to creating a world without privation, including stabilization of the population, more equitable income distributions, and mobilization of resources for

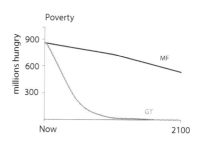

poor-centered development. By 2100, North-South and regional disparities would virtually vanish.

What about energy requirements? Soaring energy demand in an MF scenario becomes a source of instability, aggravating climate change, inviting conflict over dwindling fossil fuel resources, and intensifying the link between nuclear power and the proliferation of nuclear weapons. The GT requires dramatically less energy, thus

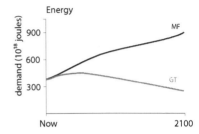

easing the way to environmental and geopolitical solutions. The decrease is in part traced to a smaller world economy, to an emphasis on less energy-intensive service sectors, and to diminished reliance on the automobile and long-distance trade. The moderation of requirements also reflects greater capture of the immense untapped potential for using energy more efficiently, whether to heat and cool buildings, run appliances, drive industrial processes, or power vehicles.

Can the GT scenario curb dangerous climate change? The MF scenario sees a sharp uptick of nuclear and renewable power production, but growth of energy demand nevertheless relentlessly drives greenhouse gas emissions higher. The far lower energy demand in the Great Transition scenario is met almost entirely by solar, wind, and other

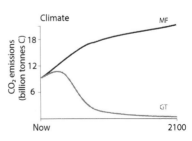

renewable resources by mid-century. Hard-hitting economic policies (e.g., carbon taxes), regulations (e.g., power sector targets), investments (e.g., upgraded power grids), and R&D (e.g., hydrogen fuel and energy storage) combine to accelerate the renewables transformation. In complementary efforts, land protection, reforestation, and agro-ecology lock carbon in biomass and soil, rather than releasing it to the atmosphere. By dramatically reducing emissions, these actions maintain climate change within manageable bounds.

How about the challenge of feeding Earthland? The scenarios diverge on both the demand and supply side of the food equation. MF crop requirements climb with population and income growth, as traditional societies adopt meat-intensive diets (thereby amplifying crop requirements for animal feed). These drivers are absent in a GT: population stabilizes and—prompted by environmental, health, and ethical concerns—affluent individuals adopt diets far

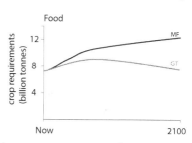

Food

less reliant on meat. As a result, the pressure to expand crop yields and farmlands eases. On the production side, practices shift from the industrial agriculture model, with its monocrops and high chemical inputs, to ecological farming emphasizing complex multi-cropping systems, integrated pest management, and other organic and conservation-oriented approaches.

Continuing in the comparative mode, how do natural habitats fare in the two scenarios? In an MF scenario, the pressures that have been driving the horrendous decline of natural habitats and ecosystems, and resultant loss of biodiversity, persist. Environmentally insensitive urban sprawl, logging, and farming practices convert and degrade pristine lands. By contrast, with nature protection a fundamental ethical and economic tenet in a Great Transition scenario, cities become more compact, sparing land for nature; and habitat protection, a passion of contiguous communities, becomes baked into project

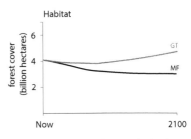

planning. The rampant loss of species is slowed and then halted, as the work of nature restoration and species reintroduction animates a new generation of environmental activists and scientists.

Last, but hardly least, in our comparative look at indicators is freshwater. About 2 billion people now live in water-stressed areas, where rising human demands and aquatic eco-system requirements combine to tax watershed hydrological capacity. Under conventional assumptions, that number will rise rapidly as population and economic growth drive

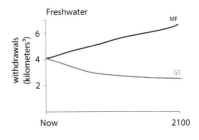

freshwater withdrawals. Moreover, climate change introduces a hydrological wild card that exacerbates droughts and water stress in many areas. A Great Transition would sharply diminish the pressures driving the crisis. Lower populations, highly efficient water use, and massive reuse sharply reduce withdrawals, and, correspondingly, the number of people in water-stressed areas. Even so, water sustainability would remain a pressing and persistent issue.

What are the larger implications of these contrasting patterns? The following figure provides a bird's eye view.[14] The left image summarizes the current state of affairs for key environmental and social targets. Environmental targets are specified as "planetary boundaries," which delineate the safe operating space for Earth; social targets reflect widely adopted indicators and goals. (The dark circle indicates the "safe zone" where targets are met.) The world today confronts a red-alert emergency with five of the ten targets in the danger zone (the solid wedges). The right-lower panel shows that, in the course of this century, the Market Forces scenario would push the global system far into the danger zone across many environmental and social dimensions, as disruption ripples across space and time.

By contrast, a Great Transition path would reroute the itinerary of the future into the safe zone of a resilient and equitable Earthland. The takeaway from the quantitative analysis is highly robust: the "big if" is not whether the numbers work out under Great Transition cultural and political assumptions—it is whether those assumptions can be made valid. Addressing this question takes us beyond the comfort zone of technical analysis and into the difficult terrain of cultural change and collective action.

Boundaries and Targets in Two Scenarios

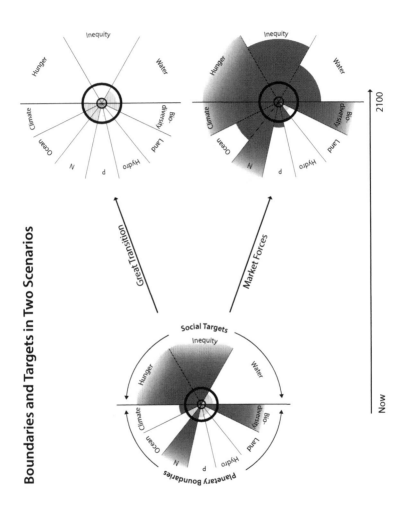

Rising up

Citizens without borders

Will we denizens of Earthland awaken as citizens of a planetary community? Hope rests with the cosmopolitan taproots sprouting in the crumbling foundations of the Modern Era. The fundamental condition of the Planetary Phase—shared risks and a common fate—urges collective responses that transcend fractious political arrangements and truncated social visions. Augmented interdependence kindles modes of association and currents of thought attuned to the superordinate configuration of Earthland (at the same time breeding the social pathologies of Barbarization).

Most notably for the politics of transition, a thickening web of connectivity fosters the idea of global citizenship.[15] This stretching of the institutional fabric of social structures and the emotional fabric of identity extends an ancient process. Eons of social evolution have knit together larger and more complex groups and nested them in hierarchical assemblages. The layering of families, clans, tribes, villages, cities, and nations places each individual at the center of concentric circles of community, balancing commitments and negotiating tensions among them.

As they coalesced, new solidarities forged loyalties so strong that individuals were willing to sacrifice, even their lives, for the welfare of the group. The veneration of idols, symbols, and leaders instilled the mythic force of the collective "we" in the psyches of new generations. Outside the walls dwelt the oft demonized "other" unworthy of equal moral concern. These contending themes—group solidarity and intergroup antagonism—have brightened and darkened the human story from time immemorial. As social complexification encouraged extension of the commonwealth of sympathy, the tenacious hold of particularism slowed the cosmopolitanism impulse, and at times reversed it. Eventually, dominant societies expanded their domains by assimilating or annihilating weaker contemporaries. On the graves of the oppressed and subordinated, historical possibilities opened for constructing fresh social forms and moral identities.

Philosophers have long dreamed of a time when the ring of community would encircle the entire human family. This universal vision has captivated the social imagination since the fifth century BCE when Socrates proclaimed, "I am a citizen, not of Athens, or Greece, but of the world." Two centuries later, the Stoics built an ethical framework that centered on the notion of *cosmopolis*—a world polity in harmony with reason and the universe.

From this ancient font, the cosmopolitan idea mutated and evolved through the millennia, as visionaries pondered its meaning and world-changers pursued its promise. The lofty dream refused to die even as the sorry saga of the disputatious human species made One World seem a mere pipe dream. But criticism from philosophic skeptics and ideological opponents did not stop the quest for world civilization, which reached new prominence in the humanism and universalism of the Enlightenment. After a lull in the nineteenth century, the prophetic search resumed in the mid-twentieth, a response both courageous and desperate to the ambient sense of cultural exhaustion in an era rocked by world war and threatened by nuclear holocaust.[16]

Heretofore, the cosmopolitan sensibility evolved in a sphere of ideas detached from the material sphere of actual history. Cosmopolis floated in rarefied ether above the divided turf where it must be built. Now, the Planetary Phase brings the once quixotic dream into the practical realm, anchoring the ethos of human solidarity in the logic of the contemporary condition—if the alarms of danger and bells of promise it sounds rouse the global citizen from slumber. As connectivity globalizes in the external world, so might empathy globalize in the human heart.

What, then, does it mean to be a global citizen? The condition of citizenship, even in its familiar guise of state citizenship, eludes precise definition. In the broadest sense, a citizen is a member of a political community that grants rights and entitlements to the individual, while requiring the individual to fulfill responsibilities and obligations. Beyond a juridical relationship to a *polis*, a citizen in the fullest sense embraces an emotive relationship of allegiance and attachment to the larger community. But the concrete meaning of citizenship has been constituted historically, evolving in concert with changing social systems.

Multitiered modern citizenship formed in three successive waves that extended entitlements in economic, political, and social arenas (at least to those enfranchised as citizens).[17] In the eighteenth century, *civil citizenship* conferred economic opportunity, individual freedoms, and property rights. In the nineteenth, *political citizenship* spread democracy and the right to vote. In the twentieth, *social citizenship* brought minimum standards of welfare. Each extension of rights followed a corresponding wave of social mobilization against traditional privilege. Thus, civil citizenship codified the triumph of entrepreneurial classes over feudal interests, political citizenship nullified the divine rights of monarchs and the despotism of powerful elites, and social citizenship was won by associated workers in their long battle with laissez-faire capitalism. Of course, it has taken many decades for women and excluded subgroups to gain these entitlements, an unfinished struggle in many countries.

Now, as the Planetary Phase roils these old categories of citizenship, a fourth wave gathers: *global citizenship*. As with state citizenship, this broader concept has affective and institutional dimensions. People become "citizens of the world" in the emotive sense when their concerns extend to the whole human family and, beyond, to the ecosphere that sustains us. This sense of transboundary identity animates a growing band of "citizen pilgrims," who sail like the early voyagers toward an imagined global community.[18]

Planetized consciousness is a momentous step in the maturation of human culture. As it more and more permeates twenty-first- century mindsets, the practical work of building the institutional scaffolding and functional apparatus for planetary democracy can proceed. To that end, Part III of this essay—"Destination"—envisions the architecture for Earthland's political system following a Great Transition. Such a superordinate configuration would draw on precursors already multiplying within the current order through multilateral decision-making processes and civil society networks. But no longer merely balancing the interests of competing states, or bowing to the interests of corporate power, global governance would be beholden to the whole body politic.

From the vantage point of the antagonistic present, the prospects for a global demos may seem remote, even far-fetched. But to dismiss the possibility out-of-hand would be a failure of historical imagination, rather like an eighteenth-century skeptic dismissing the possibility of sovereign nations as an implausible dream. For eons, there had been states and nations—political territories and cultural groups—but no nation-states to make the two congruent. Yet nationalism carried the day, welding modern states from the fractured identities of city-state, fiefdom, and tribe. In mere centuries, it redrew a world map of 200,000 territories into one with 200 countries. The old skeptics are long forgotten as each "imagined community" celebrates the prescience, idealism, and heroism of its founding patriots, and once arbitrary national boundaries are considered inviolate.[19]

Now, in turn, the Planetary Phase is rattling the nation-state order and sheathing it with a thickening carapace of global governance. But to the incredulous, ascendant globalism in the twenty-first century seems as preposterous as ascendant nationalism may have seemed, at least to the narrow-minded, in the eighteenth, before history made the impossible inevitable. True, external circumstances—economic competition, bellicose rivals, colonial conquest—were at play in the formation of modern states, while Earthland lacks territorial boundaries, and thus no "other" at its gates to encourage unity and cohesion (excluding an extra-terrestrial invasion).

Still, the powerful centering forces of shared risks and a shared fate pull against disunity, making the planet the natural boundary for human affairs. Indeed, the integral earth offers a basis for an imagined planetary community more grounded in social and ecological realities than did the arbitrary boundaries of fledgling national communities.

As national citizenship once dissolved barriers within states, global citizenship could reduce divisions between them, and thereby bridge the chasm between obsolete twentieth-century structures and stark twenty-first-century realities.

Dimensions of collective action

The entanglement of people, planet, and progeny etches the cosmopolitan impulse onto the DNA of our epoch. But the inclination will ebb, or persist mainly in isolated cultural pockets, unless joined to a popular social movement. As the bitter defeats of the past will painfully attest, discontent can dissipate and longing can wane, leaving demagoguery to rise from embers of fear (one need only recall the failures of progressive forces to stem fascism).

And yet, episodes of social mobilization do punctuate history. In victory and defeat, the oppressed, the patriotic, and the idealistic have risen up, their aims as varied as the historical conditions that spawned them. Some movements have championed narrow ethnic, religious, national, and ideological causes. Others have sought to expand the spheres of rights, justice, peace, and care for the environment, and this is the progressive tradition that commands our attention in the search for efficacious models of globalized collective action.

Of course, the lessons drawn from the experience of past movements can have only partial contemporary relevance. All movements are creatures of their time and place, and a global citizens movement, as unprecedented as the Planetary Phase that sparks it, would be no exception. Still, it is worth asking of forerunner movements: What political conditions paved the way? What strategies galvanized mass participation? What attributes attracted and retained adherents? Corresponding to these three questions, three germane factors are *system vulnerability*, *organizational capability*, and *cultural solidarity*.[20]

A stable society maintains the allegiance of its citizens so long as the powers-that-be are thought to govern competently and fairly. The system becomes vulnerable when it is widely perceived to be inept or unjust, and often both. If dominant structures are unable to suppress discontent or accommodate demands for change, then society moves toward the cusp of a systemic crisis. Eventually, if conditions deteriorate and the legitimacy of the established order erodes further, individualized dissatisfaction can become reframed as general grievance, and isolated acts of defiance can coalesce into mass resistance.

But system vulnerability is only the precondition that paves the way for a consequential social movement, not its guarantor. Actualization requires the creation of adept organizations that serve to concentrate and amplify oppositional energy. These organizations are the formal manifestation and drivetrain of the movement, not the movement itself. Their role is to channel ambient indignation, spontaneous protest, and demands and visions into forceful action. They anchor sublime aspirations in the mundane tasks of building managerial competence, securing financial resources, exhibiting strategic acumen, and generating a repertoire of tactics for spreading the message and winning battles.

Widespread grievance may be its raison d'être and organizational capability its means, but it takes cultural solidarity to bind a mass movement as a human fellowship. More than an impersonal political arena, an enduring movement offers an inviting alternative to the dominant culture. It forms a like-minded community where participants can reshape identities, establish sympathetic bonds, and invest allegiance. The counter-hegemonic culture renews emotive unity through symbols, myths, and rituals, while cultivating a shared conceptual framework for understanding the world and how to change it.

To endure and flourish, a fledgling movement must overcome the paradoxical "collective action problem." Many sympathizers will hesitate to participate until they believe that the movement can make a difference, yet success requires mass engagement. It takes steadfast resolve by a committed core to build visibility and credibility, and disarm the skepticism of potential adherents. If conditions are favorable and commitments tenacious, a growing movement can reach the critical threshold for takeoff. Beyond the tipping point, the dedicated few become a snowballing multitude.

Imagine all the people

Can a "global citizens movement" for a Great Transition take shape at the requisite speed, scale, and coherence? The race for the soul of Earthland is on. Disturbing omens abound, yet spreading awareness and broadening engagement hint that a systemic movement may be gestating. The question becomes how to help bring it into the world and give it life. The generative factors—system vulnerability, organizational capability, and cultural solidarity—at play in triggering movements of the past will need to align in the requisite dynamic for a vital GCM to take shape in the coming years.

Almost certainly, the regnant global system, already widely viewed as ineffectual and illegitimate, will become increasingly vulnerable.

The interstate order lacks the coordinated political authority to resolve crises and command public trust. Global corporate capitalism runs amok, predisposed to despoil nature and generate inequality, not foster secure and fulfilling lives. The world system, incompetent and rigged for the benefit of the few, incubates discontent that bubbles to the surface in myriad forms—and churns below it in the disquieted modern psyche.

The palpable vulnerability of the system contrasts with the underdevelopment of the other critical factors—strong mobilizing organizations and a cohesive oppositional community—essential for grounding a vibrant GCM. The challenge is no less than creating the basis for collective action across the great cultural and spatial distances that a global movement must circumscribe.[21] Even as the Planetary Phase strengthens the gravitational pull toward unity, and the Internet shrinks psychic distance, barriers of language and tradition remain, and suspicions and resentment persist.

Still, the fledgling GCM will stand on a well-established foundation of universal social and ethical principles, elaborated in agreements such as the Universal Declaration of Human Rights and the Earth Charter, and put into action by a panoply of people's movements. It can build legitimacy and draw adherents by articulating a rigorous and inspiring vision of planetary civilization. It can create a magnetic community of people by embodying its visionary goals in their pursuit. Thus, like the Earthland it envisions, a GCM would nurture a culture of nonviolence, tolerance, respect, and democracy, adhering unflinchingly to the core Great Transition values of quality of life, human solidarity, and ecological resilience.

Building and maintaining normative solidarity in a movement of such diversity would be the greatest barrier to success. A GCM would face the daunting hurdle of building unity in an era of strong identity politics, cultural schism, and skepticism about leadership. A movement up to the task of global transformation would have to discover ways to balance the need for coherence and the desire for pluralism. It cannot eliminate ideological conflict, regional antagonism, and organizational turf battles. Indeed, this very diversity would be a source of the movement's richness and vitality. Nonetheless, finding common purpose will take a global vision and movement culture that understands variety in perspectives and initiatives as different expressions of a common project. Unity and diversity are both essential and complementary.

Complex movements spark kaleidoscopic organizational manifestations, and the GCM would be no exception. Rather than a single entity, multitudinous quasi-autonomous elements would press on all fronts (environment, justice, peace, human well-being, and equality) and engage at all scales (local, national, regional, and global). Thus, a viable GCM, like the Earthland it seeks, would be as global as need be and as local as can be, a polycentric ecology of formal and informal associations under an umbrella of shared identity and purpose. It can be imagined as an exhilarating collective experiment in ways to act together on the path to a planetary civilization.

This kind of movement will not be woven whole-cloth by conspirators from above, nor will it arise spontaneously from "blessed unrest" below.[22] Proactive organizing strategies attuned to the great complexity of the task will need to navigate between the polar pitfalls of rigidity (the nemesis of vanguardism) and disorder (the curse of anarchism). But the times cry out, the need overdue, for building large-scale campaigns with the explicit purpose of catalyzing a GCM.

While there can be no blueprints, we can imagine the broad contours of a living campaign. In one narrative, it would coalesce as a network of networks, attracting new adherents through local, national, and global nodes. It would connect the full spectrum of issues within an integrated strategic and intellectual framework. It would be eager to experiment with organizational forms and communications technologies for integrating efforts across regions, scales, and issues. It would seek to bridge divisions of culture, class, and place, honoring diversity and pluralism within an umbrella of common principles and goals. Its structure and program would evolve, adapting to changing internal and external circumstances.

All this will take the cultivation and practice of a "politics of trust" that tolerates proximate differences in order to sustain the ultimate basis for unity. Like all social change movements, a GCM must simultaneously reach out and resist—expanding participation and forging alliances, on the one hand, and identifying and challenging entrenched forces, on the other. An emphasis on trust does not discount the realities of power and interest, or assume away conflicts sure to lie on the path to Earthland. Rather, emphasizing trust suggests that inclusion and the reconciliation of pluralism, unity, and vision are fundamental challenges for the birth and growth of an authentic movement.

The new planetary praxis will have many vital dimensions, including advancing systemic knowledge, pressing for strong policy, creating local niches that prefigure the larger transition, and articulating attractive and viable global visions. All these efforts are necessary but not sufficient. The additional task of building the global movement now beckons all who care about the quality of the future. The enterprise is extraordinary, but so are the times: in transformative social moments such as ours, the efforts of an active minority can ripple through the cultural field, converting latent potential into collective action. The frontline project now is to weave disparate grievances and actions into a movement of and for Earthland, a collective quest for a civilization worthy of the name.

PART III
DESTINATION: SCENES FROM A
CIVILIZED FUTURE

Mandela City, 2084

Let us pause, in this centennial of George Orwell's nightmare year, to remember where we have been and reflect on where we are on the long arc of the Great Transition. This brief treatise considers the state of planetary civilization today, sketching its complex structure, social dynamism, and unfinished promise—and, yes, celebrating how far we have come. The portrayal may strike some readers as overly burnished, but this author, a proud veteran of the battle for the twenty-first century, makes no apology. He cannot claim neutrality, yet has no illusions: we live in Earthland—not Shangri-La—where real people confront real problems. Still, who would deny that the world today stands as living refutation of the apocalyptic premonitions that once haunted dreams of the future?

One hundred years that shook the world

Our snapshot of 2084 can glimpse only a single frame in the moving picture of twenty-first-century history. That history, already the subject of an ocean of literature plumbing the roots and meaning of the Great Transition, is swelled daily by new discoveries, interpretations, and controversies. Rather than add more foam to that rising tide, a potted history will suffice here for locating the contemporary world in the context of the unfolding transition. The "five stage theory" introduced in the seminal chronicle *One Hundred Years That Shook the World* offers a useful framework.

Major Stages of the Great Transition

			General Emergency	Reform Era	Commonwealth of Earthland	
Takeoff		Rolling Crisis				→ ?
1980		2001	2023	2028	2048	2084

Takeoff of the Planetary Phase (1980–2001). A unitary social-ecological global system began to crystallize, signaling the onset of a major new epoch. This holistic phenomenon found multiple expressions, among them economic globalization, biospheric disruption, digital connectivity, transnational civil society, and global terrorism. The formation of an interdependent configuration accelerated after the collapse of the bipolar Cold War order in 1989, as global capitalism gained hegemony, lubricated by "Washington Consensus" policies of deregulation, free trade, privatization, and retrenchment of government services. In response, massive protests erupted at intergovernmental meetings, but they could only slow, not reverse, the juggernaut of corporate-led globalization. In parallel, burgeoning cross-border marketing and entertainment industries spurred consumerism among the affluent, yearning among the have-nots, and thwarted expectations among the young and angry. A dissonant cacophony—dot-com bubbles bursting, towers crashing, dogs of war barking, glaciers collapsing—rang in the new millennium, shattering dreams of market utopia.

Rolling Crisis (2001–2023). Freewheeling turbo-capitalism segued into an unrelenting drumbeat of war, violence, displacement, pandemic, recession, and environmental disruption. The rat-a-tat of bad news, at first experienced as discrete developments, came to be understood instead as deeply connected: distinct manifestations of a comprehensive structural crisis. Correspondingly, critiques grew more systemic and radical, individual angst spread, and collective resistance gathered momentum. As the crisis surged, the "global citizens movement" (GCM) convened its inaugural Intercontinental Congress in 2021, where it adopted the landmark Declaration of Interdependence, the eloquent manifesto that captured the growing consensus on the "character of the historic challenge," "principles of unity," and "visions of Earthland."* The GCM's message spread virally through a vast lattice of affiliated nodes, spawning circles of engagement across the planet. The movement became a living socio-political experiment in creating an Earthlandic community, with each jolt of the Rolling Crisis galvanizing new adherents and enhancing its clout. By 2023, movement "circles" were ubiquitous, advancing local strategies linked to the wider shift. The popular rising came too late to reverse the global tailspin, but without it, the future surely would have been far bleaker.

General Emergency (2023–2028). The multipronged crisis rolled on, gathering into a mighty chain reaction of cascading feedbacks and amplifications. Every cause was an effect, every effect a cause, with the hydra-headed impacts of climate change at the swirling

---

*   Although references to "Earthland" appeared years earlier, this was the first major document to employ the term.

vortex of systemic distress. The poor suffered most acutely, though no one could fully insulate themselves from the cauldron of disruption. This was a tragic period by any measure, yet could have been even worse had the world not mobilized in response. The GCM, its strength surging, played a critical role by prodding befogged and irresolute governments into acting on the comprehensive sustainability and climate goals that had languished since the UN adopted them in 2015. This Policy Reform mobilization quelled the chaos and thwarted the New Earth Order (NEO), an elite alliance preparing to proclaim an emergency World Authority. Ironically, the authoritarian NEO threat triggered a massive public reaction that further fueled the GCM and the politics of deep reform. The world pulled back from the brink, leaving the "NEOs" ample time to ponder their miscalculations during their long years of incarceration.

The Reform Era (2028–2048). As the upheaval abated, the old order began to reassert itself. But the generation of leaders that came of age in the throes of crisis were well-schooled in the mistakes of the past, and understood the necessity for strong government stewardship, lest history repeat itself. The UN established the New Global Deal, the apotheosis of enlightened international governance, which included a hard-hitting ensemble of policies, institutions, and financing to deliver on the aspirational goals of the old sustainability agenda. At the heart of the NGD was the push for "resilience economies" that would channel and constrain markets to function within more compassionate social norms and well-established environmental limits. Over the vehement objection of its impatient radical wing, the GCM put its considerable political weight behind this defanging of free-market capitalism, deeming "planetary social democracy" a necessary way station on the path of Great Transition. However, by the 2040s, Policy Reform's "alliance of necessity" became untenable: retrogressive forces, stoked by well-funded revanchist campaigns, grew stronger, and the old pathologies of aggressive capitalism, consumerist culture, and xenophobic nationalism recrudesced. Progressives everywhere anxiously asked, is reform enough? The answer resounded across the continents: "Earthland Now!" The GCM was prepared, harnessing discontent into effective strategy, and gaining decisive political influence in a growing roster of countries and international bodies. The movement's internal deliberative body, the Earthland Parliamentary Assembly (EPA), was repurposed as the core body for democratic global governance.

Commonwealth of Earthland (2048–present). The current stage of the Great Transition began when the EPA adopted by consensus the world constitution of 2048 (see more on the constitution below), formally establishing the Commonwealth of Earthland. Resistance flared among sectoral interests and nativist bases, but in response, masses of ordinary people mobilized to defend the Commonwealth. After a tumultuous decade, the new institutional structures began to stabilize on the road to a *civita humana.* The revolutionary turn toward planetary civilization was in full swing.

What matters

All along, the tangible political and cultural expressions of the Great Transition were rooted in a parallel transition underway in the intangible realm of the human heart. People returned to the most fundamental questions: How shall we live? Who should we be? What matters? The collective grappling for fresh answers provided the moral compass for the journey through the maelstrom of planetary change.

Now, the entire edifice of contemporary civilization rises on a foundation of compelling human values. The prevailing pre-transition ethos—consumerism, individualism, and anthropocentrism—has yielded to a different triad: quality of life, human solidarity, and ecocentrism. These values spring from a sense of, and a yearning for, wholeness as individuals, as a species, and as a community of life. To be sure, our diverse regions and cultures invest these values with unique shades of meaning and varying weights. But they remain the *sine qua non* nearly everywhere.

The enhancement of the "quality of life," rather than the old obsession with GDP and the mere quantitative expansion of goods and services, has come to be widely understood as the only valid basis for development. This conviction now seems so self-evident that there is a danger of losing sight of its historical significance. It must be remembered how over the eons, the problem of scarcity and survival— what Keynes called the "economic problem"—had dominated existence. Then, the industrial cornucopia opened the way, at least in principle, to a post-scarcity civilization, but the dream was long deferred as deeply inscribed class divisions brought, not decent livelihoods for all, but over-consumption for the privileged and deprivation for the excluded. Now, the synergy of two factors—an ethic of material sufficiency ("enough is enough") and an equitable distribution of wealth ("enough for all")—has enabled ways of living more satisfying than the work-and-buy treadmill for the affluent and desperation for the economically marginal. Today, people are as ambitious as ever, but fulfillment, not wealth, is the primary measure of success and source of well-being.

The second pillar of the contemporary zeitgeist—human solidarity—bolsters the strong connection we feel toward strangers who live in distant places and descendants who will inhabit the distant future. This capacious camaraderie draws on wellsprings of empathy that lie deep in the human psyche, expressed in the Golden Rule that threads through the great religious traditions, and in the secular ideals of democracy, tolerance, respect, equality, and rights. This augmented solidarity is the correlative in consciousness of the interdependence in the external world. The Planetary Phase, in mingling the destinies of all, has stretched esprit de corps across space and time to embrace the whole human family, living and unborn, and beyond.

Ecocentrism, our third defining value, affirms humanity's place in the web of life, and extends solidarity to our fellow creatures who share the planet's fragile skin. We are mystified and horrified by the feckless indifference of earlier generations to the integrity of nature and its treasury of biodiversity. The lesson was hard won, and much has been lost, but the predatory motive of the past—the domination of nature—has been consigned to the dustbin of history. Rapacious no more, our relationship to the earth is tempered by humility, which comes with understanding our dependence on her resilience and bounty. People today hold deep reverence for the natural world, finding in it endless wonder, sustenance, and enjoyment.

One world

The enlarged sense of place has buoyed an ethos of globalism as strongly felt as nationalism once was, perhaps more so. After all, gazing down from orbital flights and space excursions, we behold an integral planet, not imaginary state boundaries. Social prophets had long envisioned one human family—"Mingle the kindred of the nations in the alchemy of love," Aristophanes importuned—but the dream of One World had to await its unsentimental partner: mutual self-interest. The Planetary Phase ignited cosmopolitan aspirations, meshing them with the exigency for cooperation in a world of shared risks. The subjective ideal was now anchored in objective conditions.

Thus, it has become axiomatic that the globe is the natural political unit for managing common affairs: sustaining the biosphere and keeping the peace, of course, but also cultivating an organic planetary civilization in its many dimensions. Indeed, Earthland's thriving world culture and demos stand as the apotheoses of the transformation. At least that would be the view of the graying generations of the Great Transition, if not of the restless youth who, taking the Commonwealth for granted, look for new frontiers of transformation in space colonization (and certainly not for the fringe Eco-communal parties that indulge the rhetoric of Balkanization).

The quartet of principles underpinning our global political community has roots in the great struggles of our forebears for rights, peace, development, and environment. The 2048 World Constitution builds on this indispensable heritage, codified in milestone agreements such as the 1948 Universal Declaration of Human Rights, the 1992

Earth Summit's Agenda 21, and the 2000 Earth Charter. Its preamble draws heavily from the GCM's 2021 Declaration of Interdependence, with its call for an Earthland of rights, freedom, and dignity for all within a vibrant and sustainable world commonwealth.

These unifying principles would have remained little more than good intentions were they not rooted in the commitment of living human beings. Ultimately, the keenly felt sense of solidarity with people and the larger living world binds and sustains our planetary society. The global citizens of today have in practice absolved the old visionaries and dreamers of a new consciousness: "Let us think of the entire earth and pound the table with love" (Pablo Neruda).

Many places

This resolute commitment to One World is matched by an equal commitment to Many Places. The celebration of both unity and diversity animates our "politics of trust" with its two prongs: the toleration of proximate differences and the cultivation of ultimate solidarity. The transformation has demonstrated that the tension between globalism and localism, although very real, need not be antagonistic. Indeed, the two sentiments are dialectically linked, mutual preconditions for a stable and flourishing political culture. On the one hand, the integrity of One World depends on vibrant regions for cultural innovation, community cohesion, and democratic renewal. On the other, the vitality of Many Places depends on the global political community to secure and enrich our shared civilization and planet.

A century ago, it was common to speak of a unitary project of "modernity" in which all nations would eventually replicate the institutions, norms, and values of advanced industrial societies. After the collapse of the Soviet Union, some scholars went so far as to proclaim the "end of history," the final phase of the modernist project. Although self-serving and ahistorical, the theory (and ideology) that all countries would converge toward the dominant model contained a kernel of truth. Capitalism's expansionary logic sought to incorporate peripheries and transform them in its own image. At least, that is, to the degree it was given free rein.

The crisis of the world system put the final nails in the coffin of such historical determinism, exposing it as the convenient conceit of imperial ambition in a hegemonic era. In our time, the Commonwealth is confirming on the ground the counterproposition—that multiple paths to modernity are available—long posited by oppositional thinkers. Today, the paramount ideals of modernity—equality, tolerance, reason, rule of law, and active citizenship—are ubiquitous, but find sundry expression across a variegated social landscape.

The fabric of our global society is a stunning tapestry woven of hundreds of distinct places. Many of Earthland's regions took shape around existing national boundaries or metropolitan centers, some traced the perimeters of river basins or other "bioregions," and a few had been semi-autonomous areas within old nation-states.* They come in all sizes and varieties from small, homogenous communities, to large, complex territories, themselves laced with semi-autonomous sub-regions.

---

* This treatise refers to sub-global demarcations as "regions" in adherence to the nomenclature recommended by the World Forum on Standards. Although traditionalists still speak of "nations," the term conjures a bygone era of interstate wars, colonialism, and nativism that has been surpassed historically, and ought to be linguistically as well.

The consolidation of Earthland's regional map over the past several decades was not without conflict. Social tensions and land disputes were inevitable, some flaring around stubborn boundary controversies inherited from the past, and some engendered by more porous borders, as global citizenship liberalized the right to resettle. Aided by the simple alchemy of time that turns yesterday's strangers into today's neighbors, and assuaged by the Commonwealth's persuasive mediation and financial inducements, our constellation of regions has largely stabilized. Sadly, though, lingering discord in a handful of hotspots remains a painful sore on the body politic, and a protracted challenge for World Court adjudications.

What is the character of Earthland's regions? Although an exhaustive survey is beyond the remit of this monograph, it is useful to organize the kaleidoscope of places into a manageable taxonomy of social forms. A world traveler today is likely to encounter three types of regions, referred to here as *Agoria*, *Ecodemia*, and *Arcadia*. These whimsical coinages rely on Greek roots to evoke the classical ideal of a political community—active citizens, shared purpose, and just social relations—that inspires all our regions.

In ancient Athens, the agora served as both marketplace and center of political life; thus, commerce and consumption figure prominently in Agoria. The neologism Ecodemia is a portmanteau combining the word roots of economy and democracy; thus, economic democracy is a priority in these regions. Arcadia was the bucolic place of Greek myth; thus, the local community and simpler lifestyles are particularly valued here.

It should be underscored that this trinity of regional types is intended to provide a broad-brush map of Earthland's places. A more granular examination would reveal the enumerable ways actual regions deviate from these idealizations. Furthermore, larger regions, rather than being homogenous, often contain sub-regions that vary from the dominant pattern (a striking example is the Arcadian northwestern district of Agorian North America). And one final caveat: our tidy typology excludes the few volatile zones yet to establish a stable regional identity.

Still, the three archetypes capture distinctions critical for understanding Earthland's plural geographic structure. Agoria, with its more conventional lifestyle and institutions, would be most recognizable to a visitor from the past (indeed, some radical critics disparage these regions, mischievously referring to them as "Sweden Supreme"). Ecodemia, with its collectivist ethos and socialized political economy, departs most fundamentally from classical capitalism. Arcadia accentuates self-reliant economies, small enterprises, face-to-face democracy, frugality, and reverence for tradition and nature. In fact, all are late twenty-first-century social inventions unique to our singular time.

The reactionary Restoration Institute would beg to disagree. Its recent diatribe, *The Great Imposition*, argues that the Commonwealth of Earthland lacks historical legitimacy, claiming that our regions are mere perversions of the three great political "isms" of the past: capitalism, socialism, and anarchism. Not surprisingly, this facile provocation has been roundly lambasted in the popular media and excoriated by a small army of scholars. The blowback is well deserved, but give the devil his due: the Institute's thesis contains a grain of truth. After all, Agoria's market emphasis does gives it a capitalist tonality, Ecodemia's insistence on the primacy of social ownership echoes classical socialism, and Arcadia's small-is-beautiful enthusiasm channels the essence of the humanistic anarchist tradition.

However, these ideological associations mask as much as they reveal. Agoria's dedication to sustainability, justice, and global solidarity is of a different order than the most outstanding social democracies of the past ("SwedenX10" to Agorian enthusiasts). Ecodemia's commitment to democracy, rights, and the environment bears little resemblance to the autocratic socialist experiments of the twentieth century. Arcadia's highly sophisticated societies are enthusiastic participants in world affairs, not the simple, pastoral utopias of the old anarchist dreamers.

Regional diversity reflects Earthland's freedom and is essential for its cultural vitality. But the stress on difference should be balanced by a reminder of shared features. Compared to nations of a century ago, nearly all regions are socially cohesive and well-governed. All offer citizens a healthy environment, universal education and healthcare, and material security as a basis for the pursuit of fulfilling lives. Almost all are at peace. Most importantly, One World binds the Many Places as a planetary civilization. We are regional denizens with allegiance to place, and also global citizens building a world community. The exhilarating experiment gives Socrates's prophetic hope a living form: "I am a citizen, not of Agoria, or Ecodemia, or Arcadia,"

Governance: the principle of constrained pluralism

Of course, the harmonious ideal of One World, Many Places must inevitably alight in the discordant reality of contentious politics. The Commonwealth's greatest quandary has been to fashion workable arrangements for balancing the contending imperatives of global responsibility and regional autonomy. In the early decades of the Planetary Phase, the political debate on this question, even within progressive circles, split along old dualities: cosmopolitanism versus communalism, statism versus anarchism, and top-down versus bottom-up. The solution for overcoming these polarities was remarkably simple, but difficult to see through the nationalist mystifications of the Cold War, the Time of the Hegemon, the Rolling Crisis, and the Reform Era.

Earthland's political philosophy rests on the *principle of constrained pluralism*, comprised of three complementary sub-principles: *irreducibility*, *subsidiarity*, and *heterogeneity*. Irreducibility affirms One World: the adjudication of certain issues necessarily and properly is retained at the global level of governance. Subsidiarity asserts the centrality of Many Places: the scope of irreducible global authority is sharply limited and decision-making is guided to the most local level feasible. Heterogeneity grants regions the right to pursue forms of social evolution consonant with democratically determined values and traditions, constrained only by their obligation to conform to globally mandated responsibilities.

The principles of constrained pluralism are enshrined in the World Constitution, and few find them objectionable. However, philosophical consent can mask ideological devils that lurk in the details. The application of the framework in the political sphere has been a battleground of public contestation (almost always peaceful). The most controversial question—What should be considered irreducibly global?—has provoked a tug-of-war between contending camps advocating for either a more tight-knit world state or a more decentralized federation.

The debate on the proper balance between One World and Many Places has not abated, indeed, may never find resolution. Nevertheless, a wide consensus has been established on a minimal set of legitimate, universal concerns that cannot be effectively delegated to regions. The irreducible "Spheres of Global Responsibility" are summarized in the chart.

Spheres of Global Responsibility

Rights	Civil liberties; political participation; education, health, and material well-being
Biosphere	Shared resources; climate, ecosystems, and biodiversity; refuges and parks
Security	Disarmament; disput resolution; emergency planning; disaster relief; humanitarian intervention
Economy	Trade and finance; communications and transport; development aid; consumer protection
Culture	Space exploration; heritage preservation; world university system; intellectual property

Constrained pluralism is the concrete political expression of the old slogan "unity in diversity." The commitment to unity implies that the planetary governance sets "boundary conditions" on regional activity to ensure the congruence of aggregate outcomes and global goals. The commitment to diversity bars central authorities from dictating how these conditions are met, leaving wide scope for regions to adopt diverse approaches compatible with cultural traditions, value preferences, and local resources. In turn, each region contains a hierarchy of sub-regional entities, nested like Russian matryoshka dolls from provinces down to hamlets; the principle of constrained pluralism applies at each level. Up and down the line, our political system delegates decision-making to the most local level possible, retaining authority at larger levels where necessary.

In the environmental realm, the Commonwealth's regulation of greenhouse gas emissions illustrates the way the principle of constrained pluralism works in action. Total emissions are capped globally and allocated to regions in proportion to population; regional policies for meeting these obligations may accentuate market mechanisms, regulation, technological innovation, or lifestyle changes. Examples abound in the social sphere as well. For instance, the "right to a decent standard of living for all" provision of the World Constitution is universally applicable, operationalized globally as a set of minimum targets, then implemented regionally through such diverse strategies as ensured employment, welfare programs, and guaranteed minimum income. Finally, to take a sub-global example, river basin authorities set water quality standards and water withdrawal constraints, apportioning obligations to riverine communities that in turn respond with locally determined strategies and policies.

All decision-making processes reflect the Commonwealth's core governance principles of democracy, participation, and transparency; any politician tempted to bend the rules can expect to be held accountable by a vigilant public. Outside officialdom, civil society networks assiduously work to educate citizens, influence decision-makers, and monitor business practices and governmental behavior—and, when necessary, organize protests. And of course, the GCM did not vanish after the glory days of 2048. The movement remains a potent force for challenging the status quo and prodding change, to the chagrin of its many detractors, who deem its radical idealism an atavistic nuisance.

The World Assembly sits at the pinnacle of the formal political structure. Its membership includes both regional representatives and at-large members selected by popular vote in world-wide elections. At-large representation gives voice to "one world" politics by stimulating the formation of world parties as a counterweight to regional parochialism. Strong regional representation ensures that the "many places" are not forgotten. Together they constitute an effective safeguard against tyranny from above or below.

Within regions, the forms of democracy vary, including the representational systems typical of Agoria, the workplace nodes prominent in Ecodemia, and direct engagement in Arcadia. At the local level, face-to-face or virtual town hall meetings are the norm. Ultimately, Earthland's vitality and legitimacy comes from the informed involvement of ordinary people, a goal mightily enabled by advanced communication technology that shrinks psychic space between polities and dissolves language barriers. The physical principle at the foundation of modern cyberspace—quantum entanglement—echoes the political entanglement of the global demos.

Economy

The size of the world economy has quadrupled since the early years of this century, and average income has tripled. In itself, this growth in the economic pie would be nothing to crow about because, all else equal, greater output correlates with greater environmental damage. What is worth celebrating is that the pie became more equally shared as income distributions tightened both between and within regions. Everyone has the right to a basic standard of living, and absolute destitution has been nearly eradicated, with the very few exceptions found in vanishing pockets of dysfunction.

The material well-being of the typical world citizen today is far higher than it was at the turn of the century, when Earthland was a failed proto-state inhabited by an obscenely wealthy few and impoverished billions. True, in certain places, like the North American region, average income is somewhat lower than it once was. However, the comparison is misleading in two important ways. First, in those days, average income was elevated by the bygone class of super-rich. Second, old GDPs were bloated by market transactions ("exchange value") that did not contribute to human well-being ("use value"), such as expenditures on the military, environmental cleanup, and personal security. Correcting for these factors, the real income of a typical family has actually increased slightly.

More generally, the size of the market (GDP) was always a poor proxy for a society's well-being, although that disconnect hardly deterred pre-Commonwealth politicians from making growth the be-all and end-all of public policy. By contrast, our comprehensive metrics of development, such as the widely employed QDI (Quality of Development Index), synthesize multiple dimensions of the human condition. Naturally, the economic standard of living still matters, but so do environmental quality, community cohesion, democratic participation, and human rights, health, and happiness. Holistic measures confirm quantitatively what everyday life tells us intuitively: the state of world development has never been higher and continues to climb.

Zooming down to the regional scale provides a more textured view of the variety of economic arrangements. In Agoria, private corporations continue to play a major role, and investment capital for the most part is still privately held. But long ago, corporations have been rechartered to put social purpose at the core of their missions and to require the meaningful participation of all stakeholders in their decision-making. Moreover, they operate in a comprehensive regulatory framework designed to align business behavior with social goals, stimulate ecological technology, and nudge households to moderate consumerism. Supported by popular values, governments channel Agoria's market economies toward building equitable, responsible, and environmental societies. Radical social democracy works and works well. (Full disclosure: the author resides contentedly in an Agorian precinct.)

Ecodemia's system of "economic democracy" takes protean forms as it mutates and evolves in distinct cultural and political settings. The common feature is the expulsion of the capitalist from two key arenas of economic life: firm ownership and capital investment. Large-scale corporations based on private owners and hired employees have been replaced by worker- and community-owned enterprises, complemented by nonprofits and highly regulated small businesses. In parallel, socialized investment processes have displaced private capital markets. Publicly controlled regional and community investment banks determine how to recycle social savings and tax-generated capital funds, and rely on decision-making processes that include ample opportunity for civil society participation. These banks are mandated to review proposals from capital-seeking entrepreneurs, and to make approval subject to a demonstration that the projects are financially viable and advance society's larger social and environmental goals.

Small privately held enterprises comprise the backbone of Arcadia's relatively independent economies. But even in the land of small-is-beautiful, natural monopolies like utilities, ports, and mass transport are big-is-necessary exceptions. Place-based in spirit, Arcadia actively participates in world affairs and cosmopolitan culture. Some regions boast world-class centers of innovation in human-scale technologies: small-farm ecological agriculture, modular solar devices, human-scale transport systems, and much more. Churning with artistic intensity, Arcadia adds more than its share to Earthland's cultural richness. Exports of niche products and services, along with eco-tourism, support the modest trade requirements of these relatively time-rich, slow-moving societies.

So far, we have underscored the important role played by corporations in Agoria, worker-owned cooperatives in Ecodemia, and artisanal establishments in Arcadia. But rather than a single model, the forms of enterprise have proliferated in all regions. Certainly, the organizational ecology has become far more diverse than when huge corporations were dominant. In particular, the number and significance of nonprofit entities has continued to surge (particularly in Ecodemia and Arcadia but also in Agoria), reflecting people's desire for purposive work and a "corporate culture" rooted in a social mission.

And let us not forget the labor-intensive "people's economy" that flourishes alongside the high-technology base, producing a breathtaking array of aesthetic goods and skilled services. This informal marketplace supplements the incomes of many households, while offering artisans of a thousand stripes an outlet for creative expression. The people's economy continues to be enabled and encouraged by social policies that promote "time affluence" especially decreased work weeks and assured minimum income. Its role will surely grow in significance in the steady-state economy of the future as technological advance further reduces the labor requirements of the formal economy.

Whatever the regional economic architecture, a common principle guides policy: economies are a means for attaining social and environmental ends, not an end in themselves. Correspondingly, responsible business practices, codified in law and enforced by strong regulatory processes, are the norm for all enterprises. Approval of capital investments depends on a showing of compatibility with the common good, a determination made directly by public banks in Ecodemia or indirectly through the participatory regulatory and legal mechanisms in Agoria and Arcadia. Everywhere the application of the "polluter pays principle" internalizes environmental costs via eco-taxes, tradable permits, standards, and subsidies. Dense networks of civil society organizations, prepared to bring miscreants to task, diligently monitor detailed social-ecological performance reports and respond accordingly.

World trade

Lest our regional focus leave the misapprehension that the world economy is no more than the sum of its parts, it is worth reiterating the essential role of global-scale institutions. World bodies marshal and organize the flow of "solidarity funds" to needy areas, implement transregional infrastructure projects, conduct space and oceanic exploration, and promote education and research for the common good. Moreover, world trade remains an important, if controversial feature of our interdependent economy.

How much trade is desirable? How should the system be designed? A few small anti-trade parties advocate extreme autarky, fearing a return to the discredited time when "free trade" was equated with efficiency and growth-oriented development. But with little likelihood that we will again mistake money for progress, most people believe rule-governed trade can make important contributions to Earthland's core values.

First, interregional exchange can augment global solidarity by countering anachronistic nationalisms—when goods stop crossing borders, it has been said, bullets start to. Second, it can contribute to individual fulfillment by giving access to resources and products that are unavailable locally, thereby enriching the human experience. Third, it can foster win-win transactions that reduce environmental stress: food imports to water-parched areas, solar energy exports from deserts, and livestock exports from lands where sustainable grass-fed grazing is feasible.

For these reasons, the consensus is strong that, in principle, Earthlandic trade has a legitimate role. But in practice, the debate can be fierce on how to set the rules. The fundamental conundrum of world trade persists: how best to balance the pull toward open economic intercourse with the rights of localities to shield themselves from the disruptive power of unbridled markets. Trade negotiations bring all the tension between globalism and regionalism to the surface, leaving no easy resolution.

The tilt today is toward a circumscribed trade regime that seeks an equilibrium between cosmopolitan and communitarian sensibilities. Strictly enforced rules proscribe unfair regional barriers, especially actions that serve only to enhance the competitive position of home-based businesses. However, the rules do permit interdicting imports that would undercut legitimate local plans and aspirations. The Commonwealth's dispute resolution system is busy, indeed, mediating the fuzzy boundary between perverse and virtuous protectionism.

As with much else, policy on trade varies across regions. Cosmopolitan Agorians tend to support it, welcoming the economic vitality and product diversity it brings. At the other extreme some Arcadian places have erected towering barriers to imports. Most regions fall in between free trade and protectionist poles, and all, of course, must adhere to globally adjudicated strictures and rules.

In aggregate, world trade, while still important, plays a lesser role than in globalization's heyday at the turn of the century. The attention to the rights of regions to protect the integrity of their social models has bounded the scope for market exchange. Likewise, the rise in transport costs, as fuel prices came to fully incorporate environmental externalities, has added an economic advantage to the push for greater localization. Finally, the Commonwealth's tax on traded goods and services, and cross-border monetary and financial transactions, restrains trade while generating revenue for global programs.

The way we are

So far, we have peered through a wide lens at our history, values, geography, and political economy. With that backdrop, let us focus on social dimensions of Earthland, and the people who live here.

People

Earthland's population has now stabilized at just under eight billion people. Admittedly, this is a large number for a resource-hungry species on a small planet, but the point to underscore is that we are far fewer than the pre-transition projection of perhaps eleven billion people by the end of this century. By any measure, this has been a remarkable demographic shift made all the more impressive by the sharp increases in average life expectancy. The youth of today, who will benefit from further advance in biomedical science, can expect to be fighting fit at 100 years of age. And we present-day centenarians, born at the inception of the Great Transition, have every intention of participating in its next phase.

Of course, the story of population stabilization had a dark side—the decades of crisis and fear that cost lives and discouraged procreation—that must not be forgotten. Still, the primary and lasting impetus has been widespread social progress. Women elected to have fewer offspring in response to three intertwined factors: female empowerment, birth control, and poverty elimination. As girls and women gained equal access to education, civil rights, and careers, families became smaller everywhere, replicating a pattern already seen in affluent pre-transition countries. In addition, family planning services brought reproductive choice to the most isolated outposts and most recalcitrant cultural redoubts, largely eliminating unwanted pregnancies. Finally, the eradication of poverty, a central pillar of the new development paradigm, correlated with the demographic shift, as it always has.

Earthlanders reside in roughly equal numbers in Agoria, Ecodemia, and Arcadia. Current regional population distributions reflect the considerable interregional resettlement (about 10% of world population) as people were drawn to congenial places in the years after the Commonwealth was established. The flow has now largely abated, but a trickle of immigrants continue to exercise their right, as citizens of Earthland, to relocate. Thankfully, the old drivers of dislocation—desperate poverty, environmental disruption, and armed conflict—have largely vanished.

Agoria tends to be highly urbanized, Arcadians mostly cluster around small towns, and Ecodemia exhibits a mixed pattern. The "new metropolitan vision" that guides urban design has a central aim of creating a constellation of neighborhoods that integrate home, work, commerce, and leisure. This proximity of activities strengthens the cohesiveness of these towns-within-the city, while diminishing infrastructure and energy requirements. For many, these urban nodes ideally balance the propinquity of a human-scale community with the cultural intensity of a metropolis. But others are drawn to the lure of rural life, an especially powerful sentiment in Arcadia. Whatever the setting, citizens actively engage in common projects that foster cultural pride and a sense of place.

Family structures have evolved over the years to accommodate changing demographic realities, notably longer lives and fewer children. Naturally, Earthland's socially liberal ethos welcomes a full spectrum of ways of living together, with the caveat that participation not be coerced. The traditional nuclear family endures, especially in Agoria, adjusting to highly fluid gender and caretaking roles as women gain equal status in all realms—or at least are moving in that direction in traditionally chauvinist cultures. Alternative arrangements proliferate as well, notably Ecodemia's intentional communities and Arcadia's mélange of communal experiments. Diversity in living choices, sexual orientation, and gender identity is part and parcel of the age of tolerance and pluralism. The approaches may vary, but a social priority— care for children, the elderly, and the needy—is a constant.

Time

A core objective of the "new paradigm" has been to fashion societies that enable people to lead rich and fulfilling lives. This endeavor has had economic and cultural prongs: respectively, providing citizens with the opportunity for this pursuit and cultivating their capacity to seize it. In its early decades, the Commonwealth focused on the economic preconditions of assuring secure, adequate living standards for all. This steadfast effort has radically reduced inequality and poverty and guaranteed a basic income, and increasingly provided people with more leisure time.

The cultural prong of nourishing human potentiality has been more challenging, and remains a work in progress, indeed, may forever so be. Still, never have so many pursued so passionately the intellectual, artistic, social, recreational, and spiritual dimensions of a well-lived life. Most Earthlanders, and nearly all youth, opt for lifestyles that combine basic material sufficiency with ample time for pursuit of qualitative dimensions of well-being. The few who are still enthralled by conspicuous consumption are generally considered rather unevolved aesthetically and spiritually.

The contemporary way of life depends on the abundance of a once scarce commodity: free time. Today's citizens are highly "time affluent" relative to their forebears. Workweeks in the formal economy typically range from 12 to 18 hours (but far more for the pathologically acquisitive). The social labor budget—and therefore the necessary work-time per person—has steadily decreased. The arithmetic is straightforward. On the output side of the economic equation, technological progress has increased productivity (the quantity of goods and services produced in an hour of work). On the demand side, lifestyles of material moderation require fewer consumer products, and those products are built for longevity. Moreover, once prominent unproductive sectors like advertising and the military-industrial complex have shriveled, further reducing socially necessary labor time.

The payoff of this virtuous cycle is a two-sided coin: less required labor and more discretionary time. Critical to this lifestyle shift was the social shift that spread work time and, therefore, free time equitably. The foundations were laid by labor policies to ensure a decent job or basic income for all, welfare policies to meet the needs of the elderly and infirm, and economic justice policies to reduce disparities. Post-consumerist values spurred the search for a high quality of life, but economic equity was the prerequisite.

The passing of the era of long commutes also contributed to time affluence—and environmental and mental health. For local travel, we walk, bike, and make use of our dense network of public transportation nodes. For longer distances, rapid mag-lev networks link communities to hubs, and hubs to cities. The clogged roads and airport mayhem that tortured our grandparents have been abolished. People still drive, but sparingly, accessing vehicles through car-sharing arrangements for touring, emergencies, and special errands.

What do people do with their free time? Many craftspeople and service providers devote considerable effort in the labor-intensive "people's economy." But nearly everyone reserves ample space in their day for non-market endeavors. The pursuit of money is giving way to the cultivation of skills, relationships, and the life of the mind and spirit. The cynics of yesteryear, who feared the indolent masses would squander their free time, stand refuted. The humanists, who spoke of our untapped potential to cultivate the art of living, were the prescient ones. The limits to human aspiration and achievement, if they exist, are nowhere in sight.

Education

If it is true that education turns mirrors into windows, Earthland is becoming a house of glass. We have grasped well history's lessons: an informed citizenry grounds real democracy; critical thinking opens closed minds; and knowledge and experience are the passports to a life lived fully. These convictions fuel peoples' passion for learning, and society's commitment to deliver a rich educational experience to all our young, and bountiful opportunity for lifelong learning.

The educational mission at all levels has expanded and shifted in the course of the transition. Here, we profile higher education, since universities have contributed mightily to the Great Transition by spearheading progressive change in the domains of education, research, and action. In the pre-transition decades, market forces had subordinated the traditional aims of humanistic education to the research and career training needs of the corporate state. Restive educators and students challenged the drift toward McUniversity, but deep reassessment and reform would await the cultural upheaval of the 2020s.

Prodded and inspired by the erupting global citizens movement, universities played a vital role educating students, spreading public awareness, and generating knowledge for a world in transformation. Core curricula began to emphasize big systems, big ideas, and big history, thereby connecting cosmology and social history to the understanding of the contemporary condition and underscoring the problem of the future. Preparing students for a life of the mind and appreciation of the arts became the foundation for disciplinary focus and vocational preparation. Cutting-edge programs trained new generations of sustainability professionals equipped to manage complex systems, and scientists, humanists, and artists keen to enrich Earthlandic culture.

In parallel with this pedagogic shift came the equally significant epistemological shift that brought an emphasis on transdisciplinary study of the character and dynamics of social-ecological systems. Needless to say, all the old specialized fields continue to thrive, albeit with some, like economics and law, undergoing root-and-branch reconstruction. But the race goes, not to inhabitants of disciplinary islands, but to explorers of integrative knowledge frameworks. The excitement of Earthland's intellectual adventure is reminiscent of the scientific revolution unleashed by the prior great transition to the Modern Era. The new revolution transcends the reductive and mechanistic models of old to place holism and emergence at the frontiers of contemporary theory.

Let us not fail to mention that the new university, beyond serving as a font of ideas and center of learning, became an important player in the transition unfolding outside its walls. Academic specialists brought a systemic perspective to advising governments and citizens groups on the transformation. Diverse public programs raised consciousness on the great challenges of global change. Most significantly, educational institutions were engines of change and loci of action. They still are, not least through educating tomorrow's leaders, social entrepreneurs, and citizen-activists. The fully humanistic university has arrived, synergistically pursuing a triple mission—mass education, rigorous scholarship, and the common good—once thought to be contradictory.

Spirituality

The transition has left no aspect of culture untouched, and the forms of religion and spiritual practice are no exception. This is the way of the world: social transformations cause—and in turn are caused by—transformations in belief systems. Early Civilization brought forth the great world religions, which displaced paganism with new understandings of divinity and human purpose. Then, ascendant modernity transformed these powerful institutions and circumscribed their domain of authority as they adapted to the separation of church and state, the scientific worldview, libertarian social mores, and a secularizing culture.

When the Planetary Phase began roiling cultures in the decades around the turn of the century, decidedly illiberal streams pervaded most religions, resisting accommodation to globalizing modernity. Fundamentalism surged in reaction to the penetration of disruptive capitalism, which dissolved the consolations of tradition with the dubious promise of a purse of gold. In the vacuum of meaning that ensued, religious absolutism bubbled up, offering comfort for the lost and solace for the disappointed—and a banner of opposition for the zealous.

To this day, atavistic fundamentalist sects still practice their rigid customs and proffer literal interpretation of holy texts. These small groups may reject Earthland's core principles of tolerance and pluralism, but nevertheless benefit from them. Their rights are strictly protected, subject only to the prohibition against the coercive imposition of beliefs on others. Late twenty-first-century fundamentalism, a curious throwback to a less enlightened era, reminds us of the timeless longing for unattainable certainty.

In the mainstream of the Great Transition, people were adjusting values and questioning assumptions. The search for new forms of the material and spiritual, and equipoise between them, led many beyond both hedonistic materialism and religious orthodoxy. The awakening spawned three central tendencies: *secularization*, *experimentation*, and *reinvention*.

Organized spiritual practice finds fewer adherents as interest wanes with each new generation. Suspicious of received authority and supernatural assumptions, more of us seek sources of meaning and transcendence in the wondrous marvels of art, life, and nature. Scholars debate the reasons for the diminishing draw of institutionalized religion (they have since the trend surfaced in Western Europe and elsewhere in the twentieth century). What is indisputable is that secularization has correlated with improved education and enhanced security—and, of course, with the expanding explanatory power of natural science.

As traditional forms contracted, new religious systems have proliferated, some created out of whole cloth and others as syncretic blends of ancient, modern, and New Age traditions. The breathtaking variety of this experimentation reflects the wide scope of spiritual ferment and cultural exploration stimulated by the transition. Each theology offers its disciples a unique metaphysics and, perhaps most importantly, a community of shared beliefs, rituals, and identity. Some groups worship sacred objects or pay obeisance to spiritual leaders, while those with a more pantheistic orientation seek direct experience of the divine, often through communion with nature. The new religions come and go, metamorphosing as they evolve and spread.

All the while, the old religions were transmogrifying and reinventing themselves as the strong bearers of planetary values that they have become. The Great Transition was in no small measure a struggle for the soul of the church, mosque, temple, and synagogue. By the early twenty-first century, prophetic voices in every religion were delving into traditional doctrine for roots of the modern agenda—tolerance, equity, ecology, fraternity—and finding anticipations. As the transition unfolded, the voices became choruses of interfaith ensembles spreading the word and marching in the streets.

Some historians belittle this "New Reformation" as a defensive adjustment to the cultural changes threatening to make reactionary theologies obsolete. It was more: the religious renewal was a vital prime mover of the new cultural consensus. Had these institutions not risen to the occasion and had particularism prevailed, one shudders to imagine how dismal the world might now be. In any event, the old religions endure, albeit at reduced size, attending to the well-being of their congregations and the wider world community.

Social justice

The egalitarian impulse of the Great Transition has carried in its slipstream a firm commitment to social justice. By any measure, Earthland has become more equitable and tolerant than any country of the past, the fruit of the long campaign to mend deep fissures of class privilege, male domination, and bigotry of all shades. The triumph is real, but with the work of amelioration unfinished, it is too soon to declare the conquest of prejudice complete. Civil libertarians are right to warn of the dangers of apathy and retrogression.

Still, Earthland's stunning erasure of grotesque disparities between rich and poor should not be minimized. Notably, income distributions have become far tighter than in the past: in a typical region, the highest earning 10 percent have incomes three to five times greater than the poorest 10 percent (national ratios a century ago were six to twenty). The wealth gap between haves and have-nots has also been closed by paring both the top and the bottom. Caps on total personal assets and limits on inheritance have made the super-rich an extinct species, while redistributive tax structures and a guaranteed minimum standard of living have nearly eradicated destitution.

Of course, economic justice is but one prong of social equity. More broadly, the ethical tenet that each person deserves equal moral concern has deep philosophic roots. The struggle for equal rights, regardless of gender, race, religion, ethnicity, and sexual orientation has a long and arduous history. Movements of the oppressed and aggrieved have been at the vanguard, and many quiet heroes have paid with their lives so that all could be free. Earthland's egalitarianism and muted class distinctions opened a new front in this fight by dissolving entrenched structures of power, although elites long clung tenaciously to privilege. Perhaps most significantly, universal material security and access to education have reduced fear and ignorance, the primary ingredients that feed xenophobia and intolerance.

At the deepest level, the prevailing ethos of solidarity forms the bedrock for a culture of respect and care for every member of the human family. At last, the dream of full equality is close to fulfillment, and our vibrant rights movements deserve much of the credit. This towering landmark on the path of social evolution would not be on the horizon without their persistence and vigilance, and even now would remain vulnerable to stagnation or reversal. Prejudice and domination, the old nemeses of justice, are finally on the run.

Environment

We are the "future generations" spoken of in sustainability tracts of yore, the ones who would suffer the consequences of environmental negligence. Indeed, from its inception, Earthland has confronted the terrible legacy of a degraded biosphere and destabilized climate. The ecological emergency of the first decades of this century threatened to remold the planet into a bubbling cauldron of disruption, pain, and loss. Fortunately, this near calamity for civilization awakened the world's people to the dire peril of drifting complacently in conventional development mode, and spawned the vibrant environmentalism central to the Great Transition movement.

Not content just to mourn the lost treasury of creatures and landscapes, activists mobilized to protect and restore what remained, and to set our damaged planet on the long path to recovery. The formation and consolidation of the Global Assembly for Integrated Action ("GAIA") in the 2020s was a milestone in creating a powerful unified front for this effort. Its multipronged campaign—"the moral equivalent of war"—became the flagship collective initiative of the early Commonwealth, an endeavor that continues to this day.

A measure of GAIA's success has been the significant contraction of the human ecological footprint, even as the world economy has grown. This sharp decoupling of economic scale and environmental impact was of critical importance to meeting and reconciling the goals of ecological sustainability and global equity. The key enabling factor was the change in culture and values that moderated the craving for tangible products. The shift in consumption patterns brought a corresponding shift in economic structure wherein sectors light on the environment—services, arts, health, knowledge—have become more prominent at the expense of industries highly dependent on natural resources.

In parallel, a host of technological innovations, such as nano-technology and bio-fabrication, brought leaner, longer-lasting products, while soaring carbon costs and rapid improvements in renewable energy and bio-applications turned out the lights on the fossil fuel age. The "waste stream" has been converted from a river of effluents to a primary input flow to industry. Ecological farming and mindful diets are the twin pillars of our sustainable agriculture system. Advanced techniques for removing atmospheric carbon from the atmosphere through enriched soils, bio-energy and sequestration, and carbon-fixing devices have been ramping up, as well.

These hard-hitting climate actions have set us on a trajectory to reach atmospheric carbon concentrations of 350 ppm in the foreseeable future, a target once scoffed at by turn-of-the-century "realists." Indeed, climate visionaries recently launched 280.org, a one-hundred-year campaign to return concentrations to pre-industrial levels. Other milestones are on the horizon, as well. Freshwater use is gradually coming into balance with renewable water resources nearly everywhere. As terrestrial ecosystems and habitats recover, species are being removed one-by-one from the endangered list. The oceans, the lifeblood of the biosphere, are healthier than they have been in decades—less acidic, less polluted, and home to more, and more varied, sea life.

The project of restoring the richness, resilience, and stability of the biosphere remains a vast collective cultural and political enterprise. People monitor sustainability indicators as closely as sports results or weather forecasts, and nearly everyone is actively engaged through community initiatives or GAIA's global campaigns. At last, humanity understands the moral and biophysical imperative to care for the ecosphere, a hard-learned lesson that, future generations may be assured, shall not be forgotten. In our time, the wounded earth is healing; someday, the bitter scars from the past will fade away like yesterday's nightmare.

In praise of generations past

The state of the Commonwealth is strong and our grandchildren's prospects are bright. But complacency would be folly. The immediate task is to heal the lingering injuries of the past—eradicating the last pockets of poverty, quelling old antagonisms that still flare across contested borders, and mending nature's still-festering wounds. Strengthening educational programs and political processes is vital to solidifying Earthland's ideals in minds and institutions. Social capital is the best inoculation against resurgence of the merchants of greed, demagogues of hate, and all who would summon the dark hobgoblins from the recesses of the human psyche.

The turning wheel of time no doubt will reveal twenty-second-century challenges now gestating in the contemporary social fabric. These days we are awash in speculative fiction about the shape of the future (or "analytic scenarios" in the terminology of ever-ambitious modelers). The avid space colonists of the Post-Mundial Movement dream of contact with an ever wider community of life. (Here the old guard of the GCM, noting the unfinished work on the home planet, uncharacteristically counsels caution.) Technological optimists envision the guided evolution of a new post-hominid species, hubristically so in the eyes of many humanists.

In fact, human history has not ended; in the fullest sense, it has just begun. We are entrusted with the priceless legacy of a hundred millennia of cultural evolution and emancipatory struggle that loosened the shackles of ignorance and privation. Now, we stand at the auspicious—and perhaps improbable—denouement of a century with an unpromising beginning. The timeless drama of the human condition continues in triumph and tragedy, but who among us would trade the theater of historical possibility that now opens before us?

How different is the ringing sense of expectation that surrounds us from the ominous soundtrack that rattled our grandparents' youth, when the world careened toward calamity to a drumbeat of doom. But even then, those who listened could hear the chords of hope and feel the quickening rhythm of change. The Planetary Phase was relentlessly forging a single community of fate, but who would call the tune? Would the people of the world dance together toward a decent future?

Victor Hugo once noted that nothing is so powerful as an idea whose time has come. In the Planetary Phase, the idea of one world had finally arrived, but the reality did not fall from the sky. It took a tenacious few to sow the seeds as social conditions enriched the soil; the rest, as they say, is history. With profound gratitude, we honor the pivotal generations of the transition that rose to the promise of Earthland when the century was still young. Living in yesterday's tomorrow, we proudly confirm what they could only imagine: another world was possible!

EPILOGUE
TRAVELERS AGONISTES

Whom have I to complain of but my self?
John Milton, *Samson Agonistes*

All the mighty forces of history have deposited us on the doorstep of the Planetary Phase, foundlings with dubious prospects. We inherit a contradictory world at once interdependent and discordant, opulent and destitute, enlightened and vulgar. Deep fissures cleave the road ahead, while unprecedented opportunities pave it with hope. Our vast common treasury of wealth and know-how could vanquish the ancient scourges, yet a culture of greed subverts collective resolve to mobilize technical means for moral ends. We hold the wherewithal to build the House of Earth, but dwell still in a Tower of Babel.

In my home country, the "greatest generation" came of age in a world stunned by depression and savaged by world war, yet found the fortitude to win peace and prosperity. Their offspring, the now-aging baby boomers, confronted their own version of the worst and best of times in the bipolar Sixties. The Age of Aquarius soon morphed into the very different euphoria of the Age of Turbo-capitalism as the hippie's "peace, love and understanding" segued to the barracuda's "greed is good." Amid the raucous celebration of Mammon, the modern Four Horsemen of the Apocalypse—ecological degradation, social polarization, economic crisis, fundamentalist terrorism—were riding stealthily toward their rendezvous with the children of a new century.

What lies ahead? Our exploration of the landscape of the future brought, not comfort and certitude, but only intimations of the good, the bad, and the ugly. We found reason to debunk the false god of moderation that invites us to passively drift down the garden path to barbarization. More promisingly, we discovered that a Great Transition from a world of tribulation to a flourishing planetary civilization was technically tenable and socially imaginable—if global citizens rise up to make it so. These contending insights—the world is barreling down the wrong road, but another world is possible—kindle a schizophrenic mélange of despair and hope in the contemporary psyche.

In many ways, we live in jaded times. An alarming succession of crises and reports of worse to come disturb the equanimity of the insouciant, and unhinge the highly strung. A culture of apprehension can dismiss hope as a naïve sentiment for Pollyannas looking through rose-colored glasses or know-nothings not looking at all. Even professional analysts and futurists, at least those with dyspeptic temperaments, are not immune from the darkening mood. But the truth is that no one can know enough to be a rigorous pessimist or a dyed-in-the-wool optimist, if any persist. With the wheel of global change still in spin, prophets of doom speak too soon and with specious conviction. World-weary cynicism and its converse, dewy-eyed sanguinity, are unhelpful; both imprison the imagination and still action.

Dreary prophecies underestimate a key source of cultural surprise: human reflexivity. When we think critically about why we think and act the way we do, and then think and act differently, we transform ourselves and our destiny. Foresight and intentionality, the essence of free will, when exercised collectively broaden the frontier of the possible. Imagining what could be, reflecting on how to get there, and acting as if it mattered give soul and sight to the blind march of history. Ultimately, dystopian premonitions cannot be logically refuted, only defied in spirit and negated in practice.

A central proposition grounds the *hope hypothesis*: the very forces driving the global emergency are also creating the basis for transcending it. Even as calamity looms, the times are wedding the "ought" and the "is," ethical principles and prudent concerns for survival. The Planetary Phase stretches the objective lattice of institutions and the subjective sphere of consciousness, embedding the airy ethos of human and ecological solidarity in the bricks and mortar of shared risks and common futures. The erosion of borders both on maps and within minds revitalizes the old idea of a universal commonwealth as an urgent real-world project. Fanning the cosmopolitan flame now flickering across the cultural landscape can kindle social regeneration.

For now, Earthland stumbles into the future as a complex admixture of competing tendencies. Corporate-led development and cultural homogenization drive toward Market Forces. Mainstream efforts to civilize globalization push toward Policy Reform. Social antagonism and environmental degradation are omens of Barbarization.

Global consciousness, cultural experimentation, and popular struggles for peace, justice, and sustainability urge a Great Transition. Which tendency will predominate? With the destination inseparable from the journey, the only valid answer is that it depends on us and how we travelers respond along the way.

The Great Transition, after a period of gestation, could rapidly unfold in a whirlwind of change. As dominant norms lose their sway, and system elements and structures begin to crack, the revolutionary moment will have arrived. If well prepared, oppositional and visionary movements can influence the anatomy of the kind of Earthland that emerges from the tumult. More to the point, the choices we make and the actions we take now—before catastrophes erupt, old institutions crumble, and new ones solidify—are decisive for keeping progressive options open. This news may be disheartening, comforting, or inspiring, but cannot be ignored, for that, too, would be a choice.

This epoch-making challenge will test our mettle as a species. Whereas the macro-shifts of the past were slow, local, selfish affairs, this one must unfold over decades, span the world, and embrace the well-being of strangers and the life community. Our urgent task is to fashion an adequate planetary praxis and organize a global movement to carry it forward. Now more than ever, we need pragmatic visionaries to lead the way by combining idealism and realism, thereby plumbing the well of hope with scientific rigor.

The hour of choice presses fast upon us with the future ours to win or lose. We can drift deeper into the maelstrom, too cynical and timid to seize the promise. Or we can, with courage and vision, write this century's story in the language of humanism and sustainability.

The vision of an organic planetary civilization lies before us as possibility and exigency. We may never reach that distant shore, but what matters most is imagining its contours and traveling in its direction. The quest for a civilized Earthland beckons us, the journey its own reward and privilege.

NOTES

[1] Scholarship to situate the contemporary world in a cosmological chronology has become something of a cottage industry, with emphasis variously on human history, physical science, and spirituality. See, respectively, David Christian, *Maps of Time: An Introduction to Big History* (Berkeley: University of California Press, 2004); Eric Chaisson, *Epic of Evolution: Seven Ages of the Cosmos* (New York: Columbia University Press, 2005); and Brian Swimme and Mary Evelyn Tucker, *Journey of the Universe* (New Haven, CT: Yale University Press, 2011).

[2] The macro-historical framework was first introduced in this essay's prequel: Paul Raskin, Tariq Banuri, Gilberto Gallopín, Pablo Gutman, Allen Hammond, Robert Kates, and Rob Swart, *Great Transition: The Promise and Lure of the Times Ahead* (Boston: Tellus Institute, 2002), http://www.tellus.org/tellus/publication/great-transition-the-promise-and-lure-of-the-time-ahead.

[3] The understanding of human action as a geological force goes back at least to the 1920s and the work in the Soviet Union by V. I. Vernadsky and others; see discussion in John Bellamy Foster, "Marxism and Ecology: Common Fonts of a Great Transition," *Great Transition Initiative* (October 2015): 5, http://www.greattransition.org/images/GTI_publications/Foster-Marxism-and-Ecology.pdf. The contemporary formulation of the "Anthropocene" stems from Paul Crutzen and Eugene Stoermer, "The 'Anthropocene,'" *Global Change Newsletter* 41 (2000): 17–18, and Paul Crutzen, "Geology of Mankind," *Nature* 415 (January 2002): 23. On the Econocene and Capitalocene see, respectively, Richard Norgaard, "The Church of Economism and Its Discontents," *Great Transition Initiative* (December 2015), http://www.greattransition.org/publication/the-church-of-economism-and-its-discontents, and Jason Moore, ed., Anthropocene or Capitalocene? *Nature, History, and the Crisis of Capitalism* (Oakland, CA: PM Press, 2016).

[4] The Gini index, a standard measure of inequality that ranges from 0 (perfect equality) to 100 (perfect inequality), is reported at just over 50 for Brazil

(World Bank Development Research Group, "GINI Index (World Bank Estimates),"
accessed December 21, 2015, http://data.worldbank.org/indicator/SI.POV.
GINI?locations=BR) and about 70 for the world considered as a single country
(Branco Milanovic, "Global Inequality: From Class to Location, from Proletarians
to Migrants," *Global Policy* 3 [2012]: 125–134). Hunger data for 2015 is from
World Hunger and Poverty Facts and Statistics (http://www.worldhunger.org/).
On $5 per day as the minimum adequate income, see UNCTAD, *Growth and
Poverty Eradication: Why Addressing Inequality Matters* (New York: United Nations,
2013), http://unctad.org/en/PublicationsLibrary/presspb2013d4_en.pdf. For
the number of people living below this standard, see "Population Living with
Less Than Five Dollars a Day - By Country," Quandl, accessed December 21, 2015,
https://www.quandl.com/collections/society/population-living-with-less-than-
five-dollars-a-day-worldbank-by-country. For wealth shares of the world's
richest, see Deborah Hardoon, Ricardo Fuentes-Nieva, and Sophia Ayele, *The
Economy for the 1%: How Privilege and Power in the Economy Drive Extreme
Inequality and How This Can Be Stopped* (Oxford, UK: Oxfam International, 2016),
https://www.oxfam.org/en/research/economy-1.

[5] The recent futurist literature brims with portents of massive crises; see,
inter alia, William Halal and Michael Marien, "Global Megacrisis: A Survey of Four
Scenarios on a Pessimism-Optimism Axis," *Journal of Futures Studies* 16, no. 2
(December 2011): 65–84.

[6] Paul Raskin, "World Lines: A Framework for Exploring Global Pathways,"
Ecological Economics 65, no. 3 (April 2008): 451–470.

[7] First articulated by the Global Scenario Group (and summarized in Raskin
et al., *Great Transition*), this scenario structure has been widely utilized in
integrated futures studies, and has served as an organizing template for
synthesizing a range of global scenario exercises. See Dexter Hunt et al.,
"Scenario Archetypes: Converging Rather than Diverging Themes," *Sustainability*
4, no. 4 (2012): 740–772, http://www.mdpi.com/2071-1050/4/4/740/htm, and
Paul Raskin, "Global Scenarios: Background Review for the Millennium
Ecosystem Assessment," *Ecosystems* 8 (2005): 133–142.

[8] Most model-based scenario projections tacitly assume the persistence of
conventional social actors, thereby confining their narrative scope to a narrow
bandwidth of business-as-usual scenarios. Freewheeling futurist treatises and
science fiction break free of such orthodox visions, often by introducing a killer
technology (literally and colloquially), an alien civilization, or some other *deus
ex machina*, but otherwise offer little insight on the ways historical and
emergent social agents might shape the twenty-first century.

[9] The ascendance of transnational corporations has been well documented.

See, e.g., Peter Dickens, *Global Shift: Mapping the Changing Contours of the World Economy*, 7th ed. (New York: Guilford, 2015), and William Robinson, *Global Capitalism and the Crisis of Humanity* (New York: Cambridge University Press, 2014).

[10] The phrase "planetize our movement" is from Martin Luther King, Jr., *The Trumpet of Conscience* (Boston: Beacon Press, 2010), 66.

[11] Paul Raskin, Christi Electris, and Richard Rosen, "The Century Ahead: Searching for Sustainability," *Sustainability* 2, no. 8 (2010): 2626–2651, http://www.mdpi.com/2071-1050/2/8/2626, reports the results of model simulations that show the technical feasibility of meeting strong environmental and social goals within a Policy Reform institutional framework. See, also, R.A. Roehrl, *Sustainable Development Scenarios for Rio+20* (New York: United Nations Department of Economic and Social Affairs, Division for Sustainable Development, 2013), and Mark Jacobson and Mark Delucchi, "Providing All Global Energy with Wind, Water, and Solar Power, Part1: Technologies, Energy Resources, Quantities and Areas of Infrastructure, and Materials," *Energy Policy* 39 (2011): 1154–1169.

[12] These sketches draw from global scenario quantifications conducted over a quarter century. Rooted in detailed country-level data, the simulations are disaggregated for eleven global regions, and track demographic, economic, social, resource, and environmental patterns in considerable detail. The exercise is summarized in Raskin et al., "The Century Ahead," and the results are displayed at http://www.tellus.org/integrated-scenarios/quantitative-simulations.

[13] The United Nations mid-range projection reaches 11.2 billion by 2100 (UN Department of Economic and Social Affairs, *World Population Prospects: The 2015 Revision, Key Findings & Advance Tables* [New York: United Nations, 2015], https://esa.un.org/unpd/wpp/publications/files/key_findings_wpp_2015.pdf), while others project somewhat slower growth, e.g., Wolfgang Lutz, William Butz, and Samir KC, eds., *World Population & Human Capital in the Twenty-First Century* (Oxford: Oxford University Press, 2014).

[14] Michael Gerst, Paul Raskin, and Johan Rockström, "Contours of a Resilient Global Future," *Sustainability* 6, no. 1 (2014): 123–135, http://www.mdpi.com/2071-1050/6/1/123. The referenced paper links two streams of quantitative research: global scenarios (Raskin et al., "The Century Ahead") and the emerging approach of "planetary boundaries" (Johan Rockström et al., "A Safe Operating Space for Humanity," *Nature* 461 [September 2009]: 472–475). The synthesis clarifies the biophysical risks of alternative scenarios, on the one hand, and illuminates the social drivers of Earth system change, on the other.

[15] In recent decades, the scholarly literature on global citizenship has

expanded in synchrony with a globalizing world. For example, Derek Heater presents a majestic overview, including the idea of "concentric circles" of identity, in *World Citizenship: Cosmopolitan Thinking and Its Opponents* (London: Continuum, 2002). See also Bart Van Steenbergen, ed., *The Condition of Citizenship* (London: Sage, 1994), and Nigel Dower and John Williams, eds., *Global Citizenship: A Critical Introduction* (New York: Routledge, 2002).

[16] Lewis Mumford, Arnold Toynbee, Pierre Teilhard de Chardin, and others brought passion and erudition to the mid-twentieth-century project of reimagining world civilization, calling, in their distinct cultural and political keys, for a transformative shift. Although the apocalyptic tone can be jarring to contemporary ears, this body of work stands as a signpost on the quest for a civilized world order.

[17] Thomas Humphrey Marshall, *Citizenship and Social Class* (Cambridge, UK: Cambridge University Press, 1950).

[18] The apt phrase is from political philosopher Richard Falk in his *Explorations at the Edge of Time: The Prospects for World Order* (Philadelphia: Temple University Press, 1992).

[19] In *Imagined Communities: Reflections on the Origin and Spread of Nationalism* (London: Verso, 1983), Benedict Anderson situates the crystallization of the national idea within the larger transition to modernity and associates it with the revolutions in science and communications (such as the printing press). Nation-states replaced anachronistic social orders ruled by leaders claiming divine dispensation, but now, in turn, are becoming delegitimized, thus opening space for imagining the successor community of Earthland.

[20] Sidney Tarrow, *Power in Movement: Social Movements and Contentious Politics* (Cambridge, UK: Cambridge University Press, 1998). Tarrow notes that the three factors have antecedents in the classical movement literature: Marx's emphasis on structural crisis, Lenin's on vanguard leadership, and Gramsci's on oppositional culture.

[21] John McCarthy, "The Globalization of Social Movement Theory," in Jackie Smith, Charles Chatfield, and Ron Pagnucco, eds., *Transnational Social Movements and Global Politics: Solidarity Beyond the State* (Syracuse, NY: Syracuse University Press, 1997), 234–259.

[22] The title of Paul Hawken's facile but influential paean to bottom-up spontaneity (New York: Viking Press, 2007).

◇◇◇◇◇◇◇

ACKNOWLEDGMENTS

M y own journey of discovery would have been bogged down miles ago were it not for an extraordinary band of like-minded wayfarers that I have had the good fortune to encounter along the way. The winds of global change blew us together from across the regions and disciplines, a diversity prefiguring the polychromatic civilization we envision. These colleagues, comrades, and dear friends number in the hundreds—too many, alas, to name individually without overly bloating this slim volume. They know who they are: the PoleStar Project participants since 1990; the Global Scenario Group (1995-2002); the many hundreds in the Great Transition Network since 2003; the participants in the 2014 workshop that helped shape this sequel; and, last but hardly least, the fellows and staff of the Tellus Institute past and present.

I do wish to acknowledge several confreres by name. The late Gordon Goodman, back in the 1980s, when he (and I to a lesser extent) was working on the Brundtland Commission's report, *Our Common Future*, inspired me to look beyond its narrow parameters to a systemic critique and vision. Two other longtime friends and collaborators—and neologists!—deserve special mention. Gilberto Gallopín, a big systems thinker if ever there was one, came up with the fitting term—Planetary Phase of Civilization—for our *sui generis* historical epoch. Scholar and visionary Tariq Banuri, in his typically lyrical way, coined the term Earthland for a world becoming like a single country. "The poet's pen…gives to airy nothing a local habitation and a name," wrote the Bard.

Gilberto and Tariq, along with Pablo Gutman, Al Hammond, Robert Kates, and Rob Swart, joined me in co-authoring this work's 2002 prequel, *Great Transition: The Promise and Lure of the Times Ahead*, which has found a broad readership and remains a guidepost along the road.

I am grateful to the score of readers of earlier versions of the manuscript, and especially to Jonathan Cohn, Steve Kern, Pamela Pezzati, and Gus Speth for their eagle-eyed editing and insightful feedback.

If I have done justice to the journey's story, no small credit goes to these fellow travelers—it takes a global village. Needless to say, the author alone is responsible for any deficiencies of analysis or occlusions of vision. A final word goes out to you who are traveling in a parallel direction, with the hope that our paths converge on the widening road ahead.

ABOUT THE AUTHOR

Paul Raskin is the founding President of the Tellus Institute and founding Director of the Great Transition Initiative (GTI). Since 1976, Tellus has conducted thousands of projects throughout the world, working to advance justice and sustainability through scholarship, research, and partnership. Established in 2003, GTI publishes an online journal and mobilizes a distinguished international network to explore visions and strategies for a civilized future. In 1995, Dr. Raskin co-organized the Global Scenario Group, the forerunner of GTI, and served as lead author on its influential 2002 essay, *Great Transition: The Promise and Lure of the Times Ahead.* In support of these pursuits, he did pioneering research in integrated social-ecological scenario analysis, created widely used models (LEAP, WEAP, and PoleStar), served as lead author on high-profile sustainability assessments, and published extensively. Earlier in his career, he held faculty positions at the State University of New York at Albany and City College of New York. Dr. Raskin holds a PhD in Theoretical Physics from Columbia University.

INDEX